Cleaning
Closets

Cleaning Closets

A Mother's Story

by

Beverly Cole

Kimimi PUBLICATIONS

Salina, Kansas

www.kimimipub.com

Second edition-2007
Published Kimimi Publications
Salina, Kansas
www.kimimipub.com

Printed by Jostens Printing and Publishing

Cover design: Pam Harris

10 9 8 7 6 5 4 3 2 1   97 98 00 01 02

Library of Congress Cataloging-in-Publication Data

Cole, Beverly, 1944-
        Cleaning Closets: a mother's story / by Beverly Cole.
        p.   cm.
        Includes bibliographical references.
        ISBN 13: 978-0-9788522-1-4
        ISBN 10: 0-9788522-1-4
        1. Cole, Beverly, 1944-   . 2. Cole, Eric M. 3. Parents of gays--United States.
4. Gay men--United States--Family relationships. 5. Homosexuality--United States--Religious
aspects--Christianity.
I. Title
   HQ76.3.U5C63   1995   95-17671
   306.874--dc20   CIP

Also by Beverly Cole from Kimimi Publications:
Voices from the Kingdom: All God's Children Have Keys

Printed in the United States of America

To Carmen Chirveno,
my mentor and my friend

and

To Dale, my life partner
who has always given me roots and wings

Foreword

When my mom told me she was thinking about publishing some of her writing about her "butterfly whose wings were a different color," I was astounded. I first came out of the closet while still in high school. Since that time, I have gradually come further "out" with my friends and associates. However, in my own hometown, I've felt for the most part that I could not be as honest as I'd have liked. I stayed in the closet in order to protect my parents. My mother's decision to go public with her private thoughts makes me very proud. Now, when I go home for a visit, I'll finally be able to be myself in the community where I grew up.

One of the obstacles I'd like to see this book overcome is the great amount of denial that exists in the heterosexual community regarding homosexuality. An example of this denial was observed recently by one of my roommates at a teachers' in-service day at a local high school in California. The focus had been on AIDS/HIV education in the schools. Bryan came home very angry and frustrated at the lack of concern and respect with which the teachers treated the subject. They made "limp wrist" jokes about homosexuality, checked their watches impatiently, and showed very little concern for the subject. Another frustration Bryan voiced was the obvious denial of the presence of homosexuals in their own community (the generally accepted statistics say that 10 percent of the population is gay—if so, there were at least four homosexuals in that very faculty meeting). These people don't realize—or won't accept—the concept that homosexuals are real people with specific and valid concerns much like their own.

As Bryan recounted his upsetting tale, I tried to picture this faculty meeting occurring in my own hometown. I imagined that there would be a similar denial and lack of information among many—though certainly not all—of the faculty members there. Many of the intelligent, caring, fun-loving, and influential people the faculty know in their community are homosexual men and women. It makes me sad, frustrated, and a little angry that many of my mentors, friends, and colleagues in that community aren't aware—or don't want to be aware—of this reality. Understandably, gays in the community are afraid to openly acknowledge their sexuality or to celebrate who they are because of fear, public ignorance, and intimidating social pressure.

My family had to work through the shock and the questions that come with finding out that you have a gay child. I wasn't always able to help them. It was difficult for me to give them answers, as I was still trying to answer my own questions when my parents found out I was gay. I was struggling with religious questions; with my need for teenage independence versus my need to be accepted by my family; and with a lifetime of media, peer pressure, and social values that told me I was not OK. In my heart I knew I was comfortable being gay, but society said that was wrong.

I know there are other families of gays in my hometown, and in "Hometown, U.S.A.," who are struggling with a lot of the same conflicts that my family struggled with when I came out of the closet. Some families may find a child's homosexuality a subject about which communication seems impossible. Attempts at problem solving might seem futile. I feel that people must try to work together to solve problems, keep open communication, and love each other unconditionally.

Now that we, as a family, have come to a healthier understanding and acceptance of "Eric's-being-gay," I look back and see how very lucky I am to be the son, grandson, brother, and nephew of a family who struggled with me—never against me—in my journey toward acceptance, through my frustrations, and through their own frustrations. We're just a normal group of folks—the Cleavers, as we sometimes joke. I hope this book will reach out to other Cleaver households, or to the Bradys, the Partridges, Smiths, or Joneses. No matter what your particular role in the family—June, Ward, Wally, or the Beav with a twist—the only answer is love and acceptance. There is no room for bigotry, hatred, or ostracizing fear. It will be tough, but it's important to know that with love and acceptance from both parents and children, it can all work out fine. It did for us.

Eric M. Cole

Preface

"Life is difficult!" M. Scott Peck, in his well-known book, *The Road Less Traveled,* (Touchstone, 1978), makes that bold statement to set the stage for what is to follow. The reader might imagine that the rest of the book holds depressing, discouraging information, but it is just the opposite. In this book, Scott Peck gives us timeless tools for facing life's difficulties head-on with courage, openness, and love. He encourages us to use what life hands us in order to grow in grace.

This book, along with hundreds of other sources of personal reading, discussion groups, and Bible studies, has shaped my thinking about life. Dr. Peck's writing has influenced me to make an attempt to handle life's good and bad with as much courage and grace as possible.

Over the years, it was easy to nod my head in agreement as I read and discussed the theories put forth in these many books and study groups. The real test came when I had to face the fact that my son, Eric, whom I'd loved and nurtured for seventeen years, was gay. I was forced to put my money where my mouth was, as they say.

An interesting thing happened in the years that followed that revelation. What I thought was going to be a dangerous rock in my path—one I would have avoided, had I been given the choice—became a treasured stepping stone. I guess you might say, "When life gives you a stone, make stone soup."

What follows in the pages of this book is an account of the struggles I had in keeping my family whole and my Christian faith intact. By the grace of God, we all came through the experience with more dignity and respect for one another in the end than we'd had in the beginning.

This fact was gently brought home to me one Sunday afternoon a few years ago, on a visit with Eric while he was still in college. We were standing in a fruit market in St. Louis, checking out the produce. I turned to say something to Eric and found that he wasn't standing beside me as he had been just moments before. I caught sight of him a few yards away, helping a fragile-looking elderly lady up off the pavement where she'd slipped on some sand and fallen. He was dusting her off and handing her her glasses. Seeing how gentle and compassionate he was with her, I fought back tears of pride, not wanting to embarrass either of them.

Such moments make me grateful that our family took the "road less traveled." This is the path of struggle and re-evaluation. It requires cleaning closets, so to speak. It's hard work digging through the old stuff, pitching what is no longer valuable, and it's taxing to replace what is out of date with new, more useful and relevant treasures. We've never been sorry we took the risk and made the effort. There's nothing more satisfying than having things in order and being at peace.

And so it was that this book came to be. It was written in the hope that parents and siblings, aunts, uncles, and grandparents might see the value in making an effort to understand, at whatever level possible, their gay relative. It was written to promote love and acceptance for each other as we experience God's love and acceptance for each of us.

The gay community is not excluded from the text of this book. My original goal was to affirm the gay community in these pages. Now, with their contributions to its content, I realize that they have affirmed themselves just by being who they are. I hope it will lift up others who might be struggling to accept their true identities.

It seems to me that we Christians, as a people of faith, are beginning to realize that we need to take a closer look at our gay and lesbian brothers and sisters as an acceptable and vital part of our faith community. It is my hope that the material in this book will have a part in bringing people together and closer to God.

Beverly Cole

Acknowledgments

George Burns was once quoted as saying, "Happiness is having a large, loving, caring, close-knit family in another city."

I'd like to amend that quotation to say, "When you're writing a book, happiness is having a large, loving, caring, close-knit family in another city and also in your own hometown."

I will never again take for granted the support system that's involved in writing a book and getting it published. It's this family, immediate as well as extended, that deserves "Best Supporting Role Awards" in the writing of this particular book.

My family and I are deeply grateful to our larger community of faith for the love and acceptance they have given us. A smaller part of this body includes individual study and fellowship groups that I've been a part of. The friends in these small groups have supported me "in detail" over the years and especially during this writing project.

You know your individual names. Thank you all.

Some folks must be thanked specifically.

Phebe Hanson, thank you for planting the seeds for *Cleaning Closets* when I took your journaling workshop in Minnesota.

Mom and Daddy, thanks for showing me, by your example, how to love. To my husband, Dale, and my grown children, Eric and Traci, thanks for being who you are and for letting me be who I am. Tom and Vickie, your family love and support have always been there for each of us. We are grateful.

Four ministers, Nick Warner, Jack Ropp, Bob Lay, and John Martin, have made clear the meaning of pastoral care and friendship in many ways for our family. You have contributed greatly to my Christian growth, which is a big part of what this book is about.

Two professional counselors got me through the rough spots with sound psychology and spiritual advice. My thanks to Helen Bonny and Al Goertz.

Four "twenty-five cent" counselors—Connie, Judy, Vi, and Joyce-—got me through the rough spots, listening to me pour my heart out as we made circles around the perimeter of the local mall, wearing out our shoes but never our friendships.

For help in making friends with a new computer, my thanks to Sharon Martin and Carol Romeiser.

Being objective about a manuscript isn't easy for a writer. My thanks to Bishop Fritz Mutti and Etta Mutti, Dr. Paul Bube, Judy Edmands, and Carol Romeiser, who took the time to review and critique my work, so the end result would be better.

Dale burned the midnight oil many nights, long after I had gone to bed, editing each chapter and meticulously checking spelling, punctuation, and clarity of thought. Again, my thanks. Your help and encouragement have extended well above and beyond the call of marital duty.

Patricia Traxler first came into my life as a creative writing teacher several years ago. When I later asked for her help as an editor and manuscript consultant I had no way of knowing she would become my friend. Some of her own heart and soul are in *Cleaning Closets*.

To my publishing editor for the first edition, David Polk, many thanks for saying yes. I have found you to be a kind and caring human being, as well as a talented editor.

Thank you Pam Harris for your excellent work in designing a new cover for the second edition.

I will finish with another general group of people whose names will not appear here but will become known throughout the pages of this book. They are the individuals and families who were willing to share their personal lives on the printed page to try to help society understand. Their stories are the glue that holds the fabric of this work together and to them I can't say thanks enough.

Contents

III Opening the Door

IV Stepping Out

I
The Dark at the Back of the Closet

1

Christmas Surprise

Christmas is my favorite time of year. I think it probably always has been. If you asked my family, they would say I run a close second to any six-year-old when it comes to excitement. I always say I'm only going to put a few of the holiday decorations up in the house each year, to cut down on time and energy expended. The problem is, when I unpack that papier-mâché angel that Martha and I made together when our husbands were in the army, I smile and wonder how she's doing. When I get out those funny macramé Santa Clauses our kids made in 4-H when I was craft leader, I laugh and wonder if they'll ever gather up all the "stuff" they've made, to use in homes of their own with children of their own. All of a sudden, it's a trip down memory lane—not a waste of time and energy but a labor of love.

Christmas 1985 was like any other Christmas at our house. It was one week before the big day. Our daughter, Traci, was at some school function. My husband, Dale, was at an evening meeting. Our son, Eric, then a junior in high school, was in our basement with a friend, going over music for a singing group they were in together. I was in the laundry room taking wet clothes out of the washer while going over last-minute holiday plans in my head.

Our laundry room is at the top of the basement stairs, within easy earshot of whatever might be said at the foot of the stairs. I'll never forget what I heard that evening as I stood there doing a task I'd done hundreds of times, to the point of sheer boredom. What was about to happen was far from mundane.

You know how it is when you hear people talking, but you're not listening to what they say? Then suddenly something someone says leaps out at you as if it were written in neon lights. You couldn't miss it if you tried. You don't mean to hear it, but there's no way that you can't. This is what I heard Eric's friend say:

"You're the only gay person I know who doesn't smoke."

Now, I had been hopeful that our adult children would not take up smoking for all of the obvious health reasons we hear about every day on TV and in newspaper articles. However, that thought in the sentence, as if really made

3

of smoke, dissipated into the air as if it had never been spoken. All I could hear was:

"You are the only GAY person…GAY person…GAY person…." It was ringing in my ears and crashing into the walls of my brain!

I don't know how long your heart can be stopped before it starts affecting your health, but mine was pushing the limit. The blood in my veins came to a complete standstill. For a few seconds, I couldn't have moved—even in the event of a fire.

When my bodily functions finally resumed their duties, I started shaking. I dropped the wet T-shirt that was in my hand and quietly closed the lid on the washing machine. I turned to walk toward my kitchen. I had to hold onto the wall to steady myself as I went up the step that connected the two rooms.

"You are the only GAY person…" drowned out "Joy to the World," which was playing on the stereo to celebrate the peace on earth we associate with the birth of the Christ Child. There was no peace going on in my heart, unless numbness can be taken for peace.

In what seemed an eternity, I made it to our family room. As I lowered myself onto the couch, it seemed as if I would just keep sinking and sinking—into darkness, out of sight. We had just finished redecorating our family room in soft, restful, blue tones. The freshness and beauty of the room blurred through tears. I don't know how long I sat there, but eventually I knew that I had to do something before Eric came upstairs and everyone else came home from their activities. I made myself get up, turn off the stereo, and go to my bedroom to get ready for bed.

The two blankets on the bed might just as well have been ten for the weight I felt on my chest as I lay beneath them. I must have been in some kind of shock, because I couldn't even form a thought in my brain to try to process what was going on. I heard a car door slam, so I knew Eric's friend was leaving. I heard Eric's footsteps as he walked down the hallway toward my bedroom. He stuck his head in the doorway to say goodnight, and it seemed to me that he could see right through the front I was trying to put on. It wasn't unusual for him to sense when something was wrong. He asked if I was all right. I made some lame excuse about being very tired, and I closed my eyes so that the conversation would end and he would be on his way. Sleep was not long in coming. I was exhausted.

The element of surprise is one of the things we look forward to at Christmas. This unwelcome surprise, however, was one that I wanted to box right back up and put away with that awful picture "Aunt Somebody" had given us…the one we put clear in the back of the closet. I wanted everything back in the closet!

2

Confrontation

There is nothing more delightful than opening your eyes to sunshine in December after a restful sleep. Its warm glow in the eastern winter sky is energizing and invigorating. Greeting that kind of a day is like connecting with a shot of solar energy.

This morning, however, after overhearing the conversation of the night before—and learning that Eric was gay—the sun seemed to shed a different light. Its light was glaring, accusing. The sunbeams that usually danced in through the window on particles of dust now bombarded me with pain and confusing questions: *Had I really heard what I thought I heard? What does it mean to be gay? When did it happen? How does he know? Who put this idea into his head? Is it my fault for letting him run around with that senior boy when he was a freshman? Surely he's wrong. He has a girlfriend, after all. Oh, my gosh—what about Amy? Does she know? How does she feel if she does know? This is all so crazy. I've got to be dreaming.*

OK, take a deep breath, I told myself. *You don't know the details. Maybe they were just kidding around. Maybe it was just some kind of male teasing. It can't be as bad as it seems.*

I decided to clear my head. I would go about doing some task that needed to be checked off the list so that progress could be made toward Christmas. I decided to make cookies. I chose a new recipe, one whose details I could get lost in, to give my mind a different focus and some much-needed rest.

The cookie project quieted my mind for a few minutes, until I heard Eric's bedroom door open. It's a good thing my mouth was closed, or my heart would have jumped right out into the cookie dough. I swallowed hard.

Now Eric was the drama student in our family, but I knew when I heard the approach of his footsteps down the hallway that I had to do the best job of acting I'd ever done in my life. I couldn't let on that anything was wrong.

"Good morning, Eric. Sleep well?" I cleared my throat.

"Yeah, I guess so." His voice was not yet clear, either.

I turned my back on him as I reached for the oven control dial to set the temperature for the cookies.

Eric made his way past me to fix himself a piece of toast. He added juice to his breakfast menu and dropped into the overstuffed chair to eat while he read the newspaper. Current events formed a barrier between us. I welcomed that barrier. That morning the world news was much more comfortable than the *local* news. I was grateful for the opportunity to become lost in my baking once again.

The next week was a series of avoidance exercises and maneuvers. I knew we had to get through Christmas before we could move on to the issue at hand—Eric's possibly being gay.

Christmas did come and go in spite of the turmoil inside me. I was able to function, though I felt as if I had a giant holiday cheeseball in my stomach for five days. At this point, I knew that I either had to confront Eric with what I thought I knew or buy stock in whatever company makes Tums.

Eric was playing the piano in the basement. The piano had always been his best friend. He played it when he was happy, sad, or angry. Sometimes he played when he just needed to relax. As I stood there at the top of the stairs, I found myself wishing I had a best friend to give me support and a push as I prepared to descend the stairs to whatever was in store. I said a quick prayer for courage and compassion and started down the stairs. My heart was pounding and my cheeseball was acting up again. I just had to keep putting one foot in front of the other until I reached the bottom of the stairs.

Eric continued to play until I scooted him over on the piano bench to make room for me. He seemed so tall. I felt so old. When had he lost his childhood? Had I missed something along the way?

"Hi, Eric." I halfway smiled.

"Hi, Mom. What's up?"

"Well, Eric…," I started slowly.

My kids say I always start a serious conversation with "Well," and their name. They always know when something heavy is about to be discussed, so they brace themselves. This was one of those occasions.

"What's the matter, Mom?"

I just had to say what was on my mind as straight-out as I could.

"I need to talk to you about something I overheard last week when John was here." I'm sure Eric knew what was coming. I continued. "I heard John say that you were the only gay person he knew who didn't smoke. Is that true—the gay part, I mean?"

There was silence for a moment. He was staring at the piano keys. His answer was brief and spoken quietly.

"Yes," he said.

"Are you sure? How do you know?" I protested.

"Yes, I'm sure. I'd suspected it for several years, even before junior high. John is gay, and after talking to him about my feelings and my intuitions, I'm sure that it's true."

I couldn't help asking, "What about girlfriends? What about Amy? Does she know?"

"Yes, she knows. She's been trying to understand, and she's helping me through this. I care very deeply for Amy, but just as a good friend."

We just sat there for a few minutes in silence, collecting our thoughts. Finally I spoke.

"I'm sure it's all right with God, and it's all right with me, but I don't know what to tell your dad. I'll have to tell him. We don't have secrets from each other."

He nodded his head and gave me a hug.

I knew Eric would find comfort by getting lost in the black and white keys of the antique upright piano in front of him. I left the room not knowing where to find comfort.

I had told my son that it was all right with God that he was gay and that it was OK with me, as well. How could I have said that? I didn't even know what being gay meant, and how could I presume to know how God felt about all of this?

Maybe I should have said, "God still loves you and so do I." At least I knew that to be true. Ever since our kids had been able to understand, we'd told them there was nothing they could do that would keep us from loving them. Now, it seemed that God and Eric's parents were all going to be put to the test.

As I came to the top of the stairs and into my kitchen, I looked out the big picture window. The sun was just finding its way behind a passing cloud. My mind was racing back and forth, reviewing every word of our conversation.

Then, like a ton of bricks, one sentence hit me. *I'd suspected it for several years, even before junior high.*

Ryan! Of course. How could I have been so blind!

When Eric and Traci had been in junior high, I'd taken them to an out-of-town, multi-state, Methodist youth conference. There were kids signed up from all over the midwest. Friendships at weekend youth rallies form quickly and are intense, because there isn't much time. Probably because of this, I didn't give much thought to the way that Ryan, a boy we met that first day, became like a third child to me, sticking like glue to our family tree. A girl named Sara joined us, too, making us a party of five. Our little group did everything together throughout the few days we were there.

Things went well until Sara's friendly feelings for Eric began to show signs of becoming a crush. After that, any attempt she made to sit close to Eric would be stopped by Ryan. He would push her away and make insulting comments to her. When she would try to come into our hotel room, he would slam the door in her face. He'd say, "Eric and I want to be by ourselves." I just figured that all the conflict was typical junior high school social behavior, and I did the best I could to keep peace among my charges.

When it came time for the closing service at the end of the conference, Ryan was nowhere to be found. The plan had been for all of us to sit together for the final service, but that wasn't happening. Eric was frantic. He was looking everywhere for Ryan. When he finally came back to sit down, he was near tears. He said Ryan's sponsor had told him that Ryan had some problems he had to work out, and so he'd gone home.

I couldn't believe Eric was so upset, but I reminded myself that the early teens are an emotional time, and I tried to understand.

On the way home from the conference, we talked about Ryan and speculated about what his problems might be. We'd talked about him being an only child and from a broken home. Now, as I looked back, I recalled what else I'd said to my children and I couldn't believe it.

"Do you think Ryan could be gay and have a terrible crush on Eric?" I remembered now the silence that had gone unnoticed by me at the time.

Four years later, the light was finally dawning. I'd probably been right—Ryan *was* gay…but so was Eric. That was likely the first crush my son had ever had on another male, and it was right under my nose. What else had I missed along the way? Who was this person I'd left sitting on a piano bench in my basement? Where was that little boy who used to run home from school and share every detail of his life with me? I'd said I would still love my son, but I wasn't sure who that *was* now.

My numbness was returning to protect me. I had to let all this new information settle in and find its place in my thinking. How was I going to tell my husband the truth? Was he serious when he made fun of gays and put them down, or was he just being silly? Would it make a difference in our family when he knew? What about Traci? Eric and I hadn't even talked about telling his sister.

I sighed and thought about how our kids' friends had always referred to our family as "The Cleavers." I didn't remember any episode where Ward and June had to deal with anything like this—not even close. All of a sudden I needed a nap.

3

Church Camp

The week after Christmas is a time of physical and emotional letdown for most people. The decisions about gifts, food, and travel plans are no longer relevant. The presents have been opened, the food eaten, and the miles traveled to relatives' doorsteps. Everyone welcomes the lull after the holiday madness. It's a time to say good-bye to another used-up, worn-out year, as our thoughts turn to saying hello to a new and hopeful one.

The youth council of our church conference has recognized that in-between time as a perfect opportunity to get together with high school kids in our area for a camping experience. The parents and extended families work out schedules so that the kids can be home and unpacked from Grandma's house in time to repack for church camp. This year was no different.

Mothers were going through the sewing machine drawers, madly digging, trying to find the iron-on tape and the permanent marking pens to label all the campers' clothes.

The campers were carefully sorting through their old favorite jeans and T-shirts and trying on their new Christmas gift clothing. The trick was to get the wardrobe choices made and stuffed into the suitcase before Mom could humiliate them by stamping their identity on everything they owned, including the tube of toothpaste.

Most parents were thinking about the great spiritual growing experience their kids were about to have. The male campers were thinking about how much fun they would have playing football in the snow. The female campers were thinking how much fun it would be to check out the guys playing football in the snow. The camp directors were finishing lesson plans and wondering if they could survive with limited hours of sleep for three nights. I was thinking it would be a good time to tell Dale that we were going to have to find a way to deal with a gay offspring.

Our daughter and son—Traci, who was fifteen then, and Eric, who was seventeen—were among those looking forward to this post-Christmas event. Their memories from past camping experiences were good ones. They'd

9

always come home excited about the activities, the new experiences, and the new friendships. We looked forward to hearing about their fresh insights into spiritual growth.

This year, however, I wondered what kind of experience Eric would have—given his particular state of mind. He had just admitted to himself and to me that he was gay. I had the feeling that he really wasn't sure, himself, what that meant personally or in society. While the other kids at camp would be pairing off, male and female, and giving each other hints of amorous intentions, he would be different. If some young lady would flirt with him and tease him, he would either have to play along or put her off. Would he be looking at other boys? I wondered if there would be others bearing his same secret—others trying to face themselves honestly while struggling in silence. I felt anxious on the one hand, and hopeful on the other. After all, this was church camp. Where else should he feel more supported and cared about? Unfortunately, I wasn't sure that was the way it was in the real world.

The camp lasted three or four days—days that found me without the courage to tell Dale what was on my mind. I couldn't find the words. In my head I started a dozen different ways, but never finished.

Dale, you know our son, Eric.…Dale, Eric is nearly a man now and.…Dale, how do you feel about.…Dale, do you really mean it when you say…?

My husband was still in the dark, thinking our life was right on course and sailing smoothly on calm waters, but I was afraid our ship was about to sink in a stormy sea.

We had an eight-passenger van, so we volunteered to bring a van-load of campers home when camp was over. We arrived just as the closing worship service had taken place. We walked into the large, rustic dining hall where other parents were also gathering to collect their flocks.

This part of camp is always an emotional scene. The closing service is usually an inspirational one, touching deep feelings in the kids. It's also a time of separations and good-byes. There is hugging and crying and the exchanging of addresses. Then there's more hugging and crying.

I looked for Eric and Traci. I spotted Traci immediately, right in the midst of the clenches and waterworks, but I didn't see Eric right away. I finally located him on the sidelines. He was standing with a counselor named Tammi. She was a longtime friend. The tears were streaming down his face and he was hugging her as if it were their last good-bye. I could tell by the look on his face that it had been a long few days. I wouldn't have a chance to find out what was going on with Eric for a while. For now, I'd have to settle for a chorus of chatter from the rest of the wound-up campers who would keep us entertained with stories and camp songs most of the way home.

After our busing duties were fulfilled and we had arrived home, I had a chance to talk to Eric about his experiences at camp. He said he had talked to Tammi about being gay. He'd felt he needed to share feelings with someone he trusted outside the family. She told him she loved him no matter what, but she really didn't know enough to help him on the gay issue. She suggested he talk to Paul, the conference youth director. Paul had a gay friend who had already worked through some of the issues involved with homosexuality. Eric wasn't sure he was comfortable talking to someone he didn't know. When I asked him what his main struggle was at that time, he told me this:

"Mom, I don't know if it's possible to be gay and Christian at the same time. I can't change being gay. I don't know if God's going to be there for me. I feel kind of deserted."

"Maybe when you feel a little more comfortable with all of this," I told him, "you'll be able to talk to Paul. It couldn't hurt. I don't know how to help you except to tell you that God does care. Don't give up."

I had never even thought about being gay and being Christian at the same time. I would have to wrestle with that question myself. In my heart, I felt that God would be there for him, but there's only one way that feeling can be transferred from one person to another, and that is through love. I couldn't make Eric feel God's love. All I could do was love him myself. I had no control over his other experiences in life. I wondered if those experiences would be different since he was gay?

Eric wasn't ready to go to anyone else for information, but I knew I'd done all I could do on my own to help myself. I needed someone else's input. It seemed the old year was ending with too many unanswered questions. I made up my mind to make a visit to our minister, Nick, in hopes of starting the new year with some answers. I wasn't sure if he could help me, but it was worth a try.

4

A Ray of Sunshine

As I pulled out of my driveway and headed toward the church,   my mind wandered. I began to think about Eric, the Eric I thought I knew before the confrontation. My focus fell on the most recent years. Those years had been filled with day after day of projects and activities. At times it had seemed as if the days wouldn't be long enough to hold what needed to be done in order to complete one project so that another could be started.

Eric had always been a person who liked to be involved. In high school his extra-curricular life was played out on many different stages. He started by wrestling with world issues behind a podium joined by other members of the high school debate squad. In front of theatrical audiences he became one character after another in various productions put on by the drama department. He also discovered the challenge of forensics, experimenting with pieces that ranged from humorous to dramatic interpretations. He loved the competition, whether acting on stage, working behind the scenes on the stage crew, or working up forensics pieces. Eric seemed to have endless energy.

Music was another love Eric had in the performance field. He auditioned and was accepted to a community group called "The Smoky Hill River Gang." His role in this group was "piano man." He especially liked the numbers where he could pound the keys and make the piano jump. He was also in a song-and-dance group that performed at school and community events. They performed a variety of music and dance styles. We never ran short of programs and performances to attend and enjoy.

Drugs and alcohol were a concern for kids then, as they are now. Eric served on a national task force of parents and high school students who wrote curriculum to use in drug and alcohol education programs nationwide. It was rewarding to know that he was making a positive contribution to the effort.

Eric was not a stranger at our church, either. On Sunday mornings, he and other sleepy-eyed, post-Saturday night teens made their way to our Methodist Church to participate in the youth choir. Sometimes he sang, but usually he was on the sidelines playing the piano for the group.

One summer, a trip to Appalacia for a work camp was part of the youth group agenda. Our whole family sweated it out for a week in the humid Kentucky hills, cutting grass, building fences, painting, and taking our individual turns at K.P. Somehow the thoughts of blister pain fade with time, and the memories of singing and playing cards on the bus remain.

Haiti was the site of a medical eyecare trip for Eric as a sophomore in high school. Our whole family had gone, just as we'd traveled to Kentucky together. The poverty we saw there was deeply imprinted on all our minds. All of these experiences, along with Eric's organizational skills, energy, and compassion for people had led our pastor, Nick, to approach him about considering the ministry as a vocation. Nick teased Eric, saying that most ministers had a flair for the dramatic that was very valuable in delivering sermons on Sunday mornings. With his tongue-in-cheek humor, I think he also told Eric that the pulpit was just one "stage" of the ministry.

Nick had always supported our children in any way he could. He led them through the required steps toward confirmation and church membership. That part of his job was required, but the cards and notes of praise for things they did were sent out of the sincere caring Nick was known and admired for.

I had two reasons for making an appointment with Nick on this particular morning. The first was to let him know that he needed to find another student for the ministry. Unfortunately, then and still at the time of this writing, gays could not be ordained as ministers in the United Methodist Church. They either had to choose another area to serve in or lie about who they were in order to get a congregation of their own. My thoughts turned to a special young man who had been a member of our congregation several years before. He had mysteriously disappeared from the ministerial program under some kind of controversy. I questioned, looking back, whether he might have been gay. I wondered where he was now, and if he was happy.

I drove up in front of the church, turned off the ignition, and sat in my car looking at the buff brick building. This had been our church for fifteen years. We had raised our children here alongside other families with the same faith. What would they think of us now if they knew? Would they think we were awful people, failures? Would they wonder how something like this could happen to such a nice family? Would they shun us or talk about us behind our backs? I bit my lip. Maybe I was being paranoid, but they weren't going to get that opportunity, regardless. I certainly wasn't going to tell anyone. I hadn't even figured out how I was going to tell my own husband.

I looked at my watch. I couldn't put this off any longer. Surely Nick would understand. He was just that kind of person. I had to talk to someone.

Nick jumped up from his chair with his usual enthusiasm as I walked into his office. He extended his hand in greeting.

"Come on in. How are you? How's the family?

"Fine. Well…fine." I spoke tentatively. I looked for a chair and sat down.

"What can I do for you?" He spoke directly, as he closed the office door.

"Thanks," I said, grateful for the privacy. "For closing the door."

He must have picked up on my melancholy mood, as his face took on a more serious expression. He sat down in the easy chair across from me.

"Nick," I began, "do you remember asking Eric to give some thought to becoming a minister?"

"Yes." He pushed his glasses up on his nose.

"Well, that isn't an option anymore, unless something has changed in the policy on gays not being allowed to be in the pulpit." My voice faltered. "Nick…I just found out that Eric is gay." Just saying the words out loud let out all the emotions I had kept under lock and key for days. The tears started to flow. "Darn it. I wasn't going to do this." I tried to gain control.

Nick handed me a tissue and sat quietly for a short time. The news was undoubtedly as much of a shock for him as it had been for me. He seemed to be trying to choose the right words as he started speaking slowly.

"Beverly, it's OK. I've done a lot of reading about homosexuality. There's not a choice. It's like being left-handed or right-handed or brown- or blue-eyed. It's just there. It isn't caused by anything you or Dale did or didn't do. This isn't something that's wrong with Eric. He's the same person he was before you knew."

I was surprised at how quick he was to affirm Eric. I don't know what I expected, though. Nick's preaching and everyday attitude had always been one of love, never one of condemnation or judgment. I knew then that the second reason I was there was for my own support and reassurance, but I still couldn't stop crying. The tension had to come out sometime, and this seemed to be as safe a place as I could find right now.

Nick handed me another Kleenex and continued.

"Ten percent of the general population is thought to be gay. That's one out of ten. That means there are others in our congregation who are in your same situation. They may not have admitted it to themselves or to anyone else, but we don't make it very easy for them to do that in our society."

He spoke with such confidence and conviction. He was thorough in everything he did, so I felt that he knew what he was talking about.

I had managed to stop crying enough to ask a shaky question.

"Why can't gays be ministers, then, if it's natural and acceptable for some people?"

Nick looked down at his folded hands resting in his lap, and then back at me.

"There are so many different feelings and opinions about this subject. There are probably as many different views as there are people trying to come to grips with it. My personal viewpoint doesn't say that gays aren't qualified to be good ministers. It isn't an issue of qualification as much as of cooperation. A minister deals with a congregation made up of all kinds of people coming from varied backgrounds and philosophies."

I thought about Trinity. That was certainly true in our congregation.

He continued. "One of the things the minster needs most is to have the majority of the congregation behind him or her. Dealing with an emotional issue like homosexuality, along with the everyday church duties and conflicts, can split a church. It would make it much more difficult for a gay minister to do what needed to be done."

I could understand how that might cause some real problems.

Nick shifted in his chair. "It wouldn't be fair to him or her," he continued. "It's going to take time to get to the point of full understanding and acceptance of gays as ministers. They're making significant contributions as choir directors, Christian education directors, and in other volunteer positions."

I really hadn't given a lot of thought to the struggle the church was having with all of this in a time of many changes. It was food for thought, but right now I needed some help on a personal level. What about my son and the rest of my family?

My crying had finally stopped. I asked Nick what he thought about counseling.

"What does Dale think?

"He doesn't know yet, but I intend to tell him soon."

Nick said that this was not his area of expertise, but he recommended someone from a reputable agency who he thought would be qualified to help. He warned me that we shouldn't go to counseling with the thought of changing Eric from gay to straight. A few sessions might help our family to gain understanding and give us some tools to cope, both within the family and in society. That needed to be the focus.

"Love him just as he is, Beverly. He was a great young man before you knew he was gay, and he hasn't changed now."

I left feeling that a great burden had been lifted off my shoulders. I felt as if I had some new options to pursue in my search for understanding. There was still one giant albatross weighing heavy around my neck, though. I needed to tell Dale soon, and I just wasn't sure how.

I got into the car and started home. I felt much better personally, but now it was time to focus on Dale. Nick had helped me, and maybe he could help Dale, too, but a different person came to mind as I tried to decide what to do about my husband. Dale liked Nick as much as I did, but had always had a special relationship with a man who had been our minister several years before. Maybe Jack would be the person to help, where Dale was concerned. I decided to give him a call when I got home.

5

Good Advice

My phone call to Jack had resulted in scheduling an appointment to visit. I was feeling better, just having made some kind of decision concerning what steps to take toward having my talk with Dale.

As I drove toward Jack's office, I found myself doing the same thing I'd done earlier in the week—daydreaming. What was it about having appointments with ministers and former ministers that brought out my need to reminisce? Maybe it was that they weren't only ministers, but were also friends who had been through some of our more traumatic life experiences with us. My upcoming meeting with Jack was taking my thoughts back to a time when he'd been very helpful in one of those experiences, the day we'd had our children's tonsils out.

Our two children were twenty-one months apart in age, so the preschool years were especially hectic. Just the usual day-to-day needs and activities of our young children were a full time job. For some reason, our two were particularly prone to sore throats and ear infections. This meant many long nights walking the floor, rocking and soothing sick and crying children. At times it was very wearing.

Our pediatrician finally consented to make an appointment for us with an ear, nose, and throat specialist for a consultation about having our children's tonsils removed. The doctor agreed that the surgery might be a boost to their good health. He set up a time at the hospital.

I took the children to the hospital lab the day before surgery for the preliminary blood work. Neither one had ever had blood taken from the veins in their arms, and both were screaming in terror. After several minutes of trying an appeal to their bravery with no results, desperation set in. My "get creative, Mom, we're running out of time" mode kicked in. If all else fails, bargain.

"OK, kids, I'll make a deal with you." I had their attention. Deals always get results in kid-negotiating. "If your blood comes out red, we'll get ice cream on the way home. If it comes out green, you have to eat a can of spinach."

Mission accomplished. The spinach was reserved for Popeye and we stopped for ice cream on our way home.

The surgeries were scheduled early in the day. One was at eight in the morning and the other at nine. The kids had kept each other company in the hospital room overnight, and we showed up with the sunrise on the day of the procedure.

We had only been in their room a few minutes when Jack showed up to keep us company while we waited. He was always there for us and anyone else in the congregation who needed him. He was cheerful and casual, hands in his pockets, making light conversation. He always seemed to know what to say and how to say it. He helped me to stay calm when they wheeled four-year-old Traci off to the great white operating room for her surgery. She seemed so small and fragile, and I wasn't feeling like the Rock of Gibraltar myself.

He understood when six-year-old Eric was found huddled in a corner of the bathroom, terrified after seeing his little sister taken off to places unknown. Jack asked a nurse if she could give Eric his pre-surgery shot a little early to calm him and ease his fears. He didn't leave until I was settled down after seeing my pale and swollen little children returned to their places in the pediatric ward after the surgery was over.

Now, eleven years later, Jack was still supporting friends who needed him, but he was selling insurance for a living. He was still a friend of our family, and had an especially good rapport with Dale. They had lunch together from time to time just to chat and catch up on things. He was as close a friend to my husband as anyone I could think of. I was glad I'd set up an appointment to talk with him.

As I walked into Jack's office, it seemed like a replay of my meeting with Nick. Nick had helped me to come to grips with some issues connected with having a gay son, but now I needed help figuring out how to tell Dale. I got a warm welcome. Jack closed the door.

I jumped right in. "Jack, I have a problem I hope you can help me with. It has to do with Dale."

By the tone of my voice, Jack was probably wondering if I'd come to him for marriage counseling. I soon let him know that wasn't the case.

"I have something to tell him and I don't think it is going to go over very well. I don't quite know how to handle it."

"What's up?" He gave me his full attention.

"I found out accidentally that Eric is gay. When I confronted him, he said it was true. I've been mulling this over in my head for a few weeks and am feeling better about it myself, but I'm not sure how to tell Dale. I don't know how he'll react. You know him. You can see this from a man's perspective. What do you think I should do?"

"Hmmm, that's a tough one. Are you sure Eric knows what he is talking about?"

"Eric assured me that it's true. He says he knows his feelings and trusts them.

Why would he make up something like that?"

Jack was staring at his desktop and tapping a pencil in a steady rhythm.

"Being gay is not what you'd call a normal thing. At least, our society doesn't accept it very easily," he began, and the words startled me: Is that what Dale would think? Would society's opinion win out over family ties? Lost in these disturbing thoughts, I suddenly realized that Jack was talking to me and I forced myself back to our conversation. "If it were my son," he was saying, "I'd get my hands on everything I could find to read on the subject of homosexuality. I'd become informed. I'd want to know what the doctors say, what psychiatrists say, and what the church says. You might even have to defend Eric someday. I'd sure get the facts if it were me. Can you tell me more about how Eric feels and why he's so sure he's gay? I don't know a lot about that whole thing myself."

I filled him in on the conversation I'd overheard before Christmas, and how things had gone when I'd confronted Eric with my questions. I told him I'd talked to Nick and was feeling better because of the basic information he'd given me, but really couldn't say I was very well versed on the subject myself.

"It sounds like gathering information might be the first step," Jack repeated. "I'm not sure how Dale will react, but it would probably help if you had some facts to give him. It's a tough call. He might surprise you, though. You know I'll be available if you need me."

I thanked him for his help and his input and promised to let him know how things went. I left his office and walked toward my car, but the phrase *not what you'd call a normal thing* kept running through my head over and over again, despite my efforts to push it away. It was then I realized that I hadn't wanted to face my own doubts. My fear that this indeed was not a normal thing kept resurfacing. One thing I did know, however, was that the best way to deal with fear was education.

I knew that Jack's advice about reading all I could find on the subject was perfect for me. I don't know why I hadn't thought of it myself. All my life, I'd learned what I needed to know by reading books. I wondered where the best place to start would be. The local library would probably have plenty of information, and it wouldn't cost anything. I would have what I needed in order to be informed and to inform Dale. Perhaps I could look forward to understanding this new thing about my son a little better in the process. Maybe I could even find something that would be helpful to Eric himself. I was getting excited and even feeling somewhat optimistic. Then I stopped short. It's a good thing no one was behind me on the sidewalk, or there would have been a collision.

I was picturing myself wandering in and out of the stacks at the library with my arms loaded down with books on homosexuality. Good grief! How was I going to explain the books to the librarian? I know her! How was I going to pull this off? It was a relatively small town, and I was not anonymous. People don't understand this sort of thing. The librarian's son is in Eric's class at school.

What would she think? This wasn't going to be as easy as I'd been thinking. I felt the beginning of Excedrin headache number 999 coming on. There had to be a way of dealing with this, but I couldn't think of it at that moment. I decided to run the less stressful errands I had listed for the day, and hope that an idea would hit me in the process. That was all I could do for now.

When I was back in the pediatric ward at the hospital eleven years before, having my small children's tonsils removed, I'd thought I was having trauma. Now, in the face of having to start digging into a subject like homosexuality, tonsils were a piece of cake. That must be what people mean by "the good old days."

6

For Better or Worse

Dale and I had had nineteen years of "good old days" since we'd first said our marriage vows in 1966. *For better or worse, for richer or poorer, in sickness and in health.* How many times had Dale and I repeated those words and teased each other when one of us had done something stupid in our marriage?

We would laugh and say, "You still have to love me. Remember—for better or worse."

The phrase had covered lots of situations over the years, as well as all of those character flaws that none of us see when we enter blindly into young love.

Why, then, had it turned out to be so difficult for me to tell Dale that he had a gay son? Did I really think he would withdraw his love from Eric? I certainly couldn't see him throwing our firstborn out into the street with no place to go. He wasn't like that.

Maybe I was afraid he would blame me. I had a degree in family and child development, credentials to teach nursery school children. He had trusted me to make most of the parenting decisions that had guided our kids through their childhoods. What if my guidelines had been wrong? The philosophy I had drawn from my education was that it was OK to let boys have teddy bears. Teach them to nurture so that they will be good fathers. Let the girls play sports if they're interested. The world is a competitive place, and women need to be able to hold their own. Had I unknowingly caused this "condition" in my son? Nick had said I hadn't, but I couldn't help doubting.

At this stage of the game it was all academic, anyway. It had been three weeks since Christmas, and my nerves couldn't hold out much longer.

In a bookstore I had accidentally run across a book that turned out to be very helpful in my preparation for telling Dale. The book was by Gloria Guss Back and was entitled *Are You Still My Mother? Are You Still My Family?* (Warner Books, 1985).

I read the book during the day when everyone was gone and I was alone at home. I'd read as far as I could before someone came home from school or work and I had to quit. Then I'd bury the book deep beneath a pile of magazines in

21

the basket beside my chair. I felt a little like a criminal, but I hoped that the need for secrecy would be temporary. The book was the first concrete source of knowledge I'd found. The information was helpful as well as comforting. It was worth the effort.

Ms. Back shared her personal story concerning her son Kenny's disclosure that he was gay. She shared the shock, the guilt, the anger, and the feeling of separation as she worked through her experience. She asked the same hard questions I was asking, except she had found some answers, and I was hungry for the nourishment they were to provide me.

She asked if homosexuality was normal. She asked this of a licensed psychiatrist who told her that the American Psychiatric Association had taken homosexuality off the list of mental disorders in 1973. He also told her that the American Psychological Association had declared that homosexuals were competent, reliable, stable, and functional in society, as well as in their vocations.

Somehow, having someone from the medical community confirm that information was of great comfort to me.

Ms. Back also asked, What causes homosexuality? Is there a cure? Is it just a phase? Can a person be changed? Although Nick had touched on these questions, I welcomed a second opinion. She found that much research had been done in search of the answers concerning the cause of homosexual orientation. Some progress had been made, but there was no conclusive evidence giving us clear-cut information about the cause. Concerning orientation changes, she wrote that most therapists and psychiatrists have been unable to convert their homosexual clients and patients to heterosexual orientations, which gives us strong evidence that it is not a passing phase and that any attempts to change that orientation would be futile, even harmful.

Chalk one up for Nick.

Ms. Back and I shared other concerns, such as promiscuity and stability. We all want our children—gay or straight—to have stable, meaningful relationships, especially in this time of the AIDS epidemic.

The author pointed out that sexual lifestyles can vary from one end of the promiscuity scale to the other, no matter what our children's orientations. That is a concern for all parents. Each adult child must make responsible decisions about relationships, but there is no reason why homosexuals can't have stable, committed ones, just like heterosexuals. There are no guarantees for anyone in relationships. That is evident from the high divorce rate in our society.

I thought about this information as it applied to Eric, and it made sense. He had always treated people with respect and consideration in romantic situations before. Why would he suddenly become some kind of monster in the way he dealt with others now?

We shared another concern. I'd seen enough programs on television to know that there was prejudice and gay-bashing going on out there in the real world.

Was Eric safe? Would he be shunned or hurt if people knew he was gay? Would it affect his acting career?

Ms. Back's research led her to the conclusion that there would always be discrimination and fear in society, whether we like it or not. That is what makes education and information about the subject of homosexuality so important. There is still no guarantee of freedom from it, but the more we know, the better we understand.

Well, I was doing my share toward education, but not by choice. Maybe some good could come out of being forced to deal with something I wouldn't have given a second thought otherwise.

The rest of the book was made up of interviews with the families of other gay children—families who were dealing with the same issues we were—and with the gay children themselves. Reading the interviews, I felt as if I were on a roller coaster ride. I'd go soaring to the top of the ride as I read encouraging stories of love and acceptance. Then my emotions would crash to the bottom as I encountered the stories of families suffering, unable to cope, estranged and hostile.

There was hope in that Ms. Back eventually set up workshops to help families learn and feel supported. She was able to help by sharing her knowledge with others who were also trying to cope. Her efforts resulted in better understanding for all who were willing to struggle and come to grips with their individual situations.

I almost felt as if this mother knew my secret. We had shared thoughts and concerns by sharing this book. One thing I knew for sure after reading the different accounts of acceptance and rejection in her book: we had to work toward acceptance in our family.

Along with giving me more personal knowledge, the information in the book had equipped me with what I needed in order to approach my husband. We would be traveling out of town for a meeting on the weekend. I would tell him about Eric then.

We were on the road early on Saturday morning. Dale was in high spirits, looking forward to getting away. I hoped that wouldn't change. The time had come when I could wait no longer. I had his full attention in the car. He couldn't leave, he couldn't ignore me, he couldn't hide behind the newspaper. We could just have it out. I was ready. How bad could it be, anyway?

I waited until we'd been on the road for an hour or so. We'd made all the necessary arrangements for pets and mail and had had time to settle down from our preparations for the trip.

The music from the radio had filled the silence in the car for the first part of the trip. Finally, I reached for the control knob and turned it off. Dale continued to keep his eyes on the road. I often tired of the radio in the car, so it wasn't unusual for me to switch it off.

My head was pounding and my stomach was in a knot. I should have been used to that by now.

"Dale." Why did that sound so formal to me? We'd never called each other by pet names before, but somehow I needed something softer sounding now.

"Uh huh?"

"I need to talk to you about something."

"Shoot."

You or me? I thought.

"I found out something just before Christmas, and I've been trying to figure out how to tell you about it."

I don't know what he was thinking, but it could have covered anything from a thousand-dollar error in the checkbook to cancer.

"What is it?"

I had his attention.

"I found out Eric is gay."

His reaction was immediate, spontaneous, and shocking.

"That doesn't surprise me. I've thought for a long time that might be a possibility."

I turned and stared at him.

"What? What did you say?" If I'd been driving, we'd have been in the ditch.

"I said, no big deal. As long as he isn't holding hands with some guy or kissing him in front of me, I have no problem with it."

I was furious. I didn't normally have trouble with high blood pressure, but you can be sure it was high then.

"Do you have any idea what I have been through this past month?" Of course he had no way of knowing that, but then we don't have to be reasonable during a fit of anger, do we? "I've had visions of terrible confrontations and separations in our family. I've imagined us torn apart at the seams. I've been ready to defend myself from blame and guilt for causing it."

I realized I wasn't breathing. I had to stop a second to inhale. Then I went on.

"All you have to say is 'No big deal'? What about all of your put-down jokes and making fun of the limp wrist?"

My husband was looking at me as if I were a mad dog. I concede that I might have been frothing a little.

"I was just kidding around. I'm sorry if my response wasn't what you expected."

The only thing I could do was claim my right to clam up and pout for a while. How could he have done this to me? Of *course* I couldn't have done this to myself. The thing that had thrown me off, in this case, was expecting the "worse" and getting the "better." I wasn't prepared for that.

I would let him know how much I appreciated his attitude later, but for a few minutes I just needed to recover. I reached over and turned the radio back on, welcoming the music that filled the car and the relief that filled me. Now we could go forward together, facing whatever lay ahead—*for better or worse.*

II
Turning on the Light

7

Gay Book-of-the-Month Club

To me, there's a big difference between secrets and confidences. I'd always prided myself in being trustworthy to keep a friend's confidence. Somehow, that was a positive thing, kind of sacred, a gift to be treasured and protected. A secret, on the other hand, should be hidden, guarded against discovery, and sometimes, clouded in shame.

Being able to bring Eric's secret out into the open by sharing it with Dale had turned it into a confidence and made it much easier to talk about. It was a great relief. His acceptance was conditional, however, in that he'd said he didn't want to see any open display of affection between Eric and another male—no hand-holding or gazing into one another's eyes. I hadn't really thought about that aspect of the situation but, to be honest, I guess I felt that way, too. It would be uncomfortable. We certainly weren't used to seeing that. At this point, there was no other male to consider, though, so for now we would concentrate on learning what we could about this new and foreign phenomenon in our life.

Dale's type of reading material usually consisted of the newspaper, professional journals, and biographies of famous people in whom he was interested. However, in light of the new information I'd dropped in his lap, he agreed to read "the book," as it was to become known in our household. On my recommendation, he began exploring the pages of *Are You Still My Mother? Are You Still My Family?* As he read, he agreed with me that it was a helpful and well-written book. There was much information he'd never even considered before.

The reading was helpful to Dale and me, but we wondered if counseling, in addition to the reading, might be beneficial. Eric said he had questions about being gay that a counselor might be able to help him with. He was willing to try it if we were. It was obvious that he was wrestling with some difficult issues himself. We decided to call the person Nick had recommended when I first asked him about seeking help. We'd never gone for any kind of counseling before, but the three of us decided it might help us to gain some insights and answers. We still weren't sure it wasn't someone's fault. If it was, we needed to work through that. Those doubts were hard to shake. We weren't sure what the future had in store for us. Perhaps we could get some tools for dealing with whatever was ahead. I called and made an appointment.

Al, the counselor, respected our request that he not take us in the direction of trying to change Eric from gay to straight. Al did question Eric to find out how he had arrived at the conclusion that he was gay. He seemed to respect the information he was given and was quite open and accepting of what each of us had to say. All through the sessions, though, I kept feeling as if the counselor was the one who was having trouble accepting Eric's gayness. There was an underlying sense that he struggled because Eric didn't fit the gay stereotype. It was just a "gut" feeling, but my radar was saying that he was personally doubting that Eric was indeed gay. It was tempting to become less confident of our own position on the matter and change our plan from accepting Eric to trying to change him. Still, I just couldn't shake the thought that a person has to know how he feels in his heart, and we had to go on Eric's feelings.

Al did tell us at a later, private session, that he was confused on a couple of issues. Eric and his girlfriend Amy were so closely bonded in their relationship that it made Al wonder if our son was really gay or just having gay fantasies—not too uncommon in teenage boys.

That aspect of the situation had me confused, too. It made me angry that the nurturing and affectionate qualities I'd seen Eric show Amy wouldn't be enjoyed by a wife in a family situation. I felt a very real loss where that was concerned.

The other thing making Al doubtful was that the low self-esteem he often saw in gay clients was not evident in Eric's counseling sessions. Perhaps that was because so many other gays had been kicked out of their homes and told that they were the scum of the earth by their families and by society. In those cases, it was inevitable that they would struggle with their own self-worth.

Even though there were some doubts left after the sessions were over, we decided not to push Eric. We would give him some time and space to see what developed.

We came away from counseling with some helpful communication tools, just as we'd hoped to do. Al had helped us to lay a solid foundation from which to pursue our family relationships. We had established our need for openness and respect between husband and wife, between parents and offspring. We did tell Eric that if he ever realized he was mistaken, we hoped he would admit that to himself and to us. We wanted that point to be clear. He agreed.

I'd made it over three hurdles so far: confronting Eric, telling my husband, and going for counseling. Now it was time to seek out my next source of information and strength—the library. I'd put it off long enough. "The book" had been helpful, but there had to be more good information out there. I would see what other reading materials were available.

I walked through the heavy glass doors into the place known for its available wealth of knowledge and information. I wondered what it would be like if the librarian could sit on her high stool behind the check-out counter and read minds as people walked through those glass doors. There must be a million different thoughts and ideas floating around in the spaces above all of those stacks of books and magazines. I was grateful that no such technology was available to librarians at this time.

I walked toward the card catalogue and found the *h's,* and then the section on homosexuality. I was holding my breath, hoping no one would show up looking for information on *hormones* or something. Mine must have been running rampant, as it was very hot where I was standing.

I was surprised at how many titles there were on homosexuality. There were further references to the subject of lesbianism. I thought I would put that on hold for now, but might look into it later. I chose the titles that seemed to deal with family issues and the process of becoming more informed. I copied down a dozen or so possibilities and began my search.

A surprising fact became evident as I combed the library shelves trying to match code numbers with specific books of interest. Most of the titles I'd chosen to read concerning families with gay children were checked out. I had a terrible time finding even two that I could take home. That made a strong statement that was very reassuring to me. We were not alone in this. There were others in our community who were dealing with the situation, too. It was kind of like we all belonged to a secret "Gay Book-of-the-Month Club." A part of me wanted to go through the library files to find out who these other people were, so I could talk to them. Another part of me was afraid to know. I was still forming my opinions about all of this, and I felt safer sticking with my family and dealing with people I knew and cared about. Someday, I might like to know other families in our situation, but for now I'd stick with the familiar.

There were two books that were destined to go home with me this time. One was *Now That You Know: What Every Parent Should Know About Homosexuality* (Harcourt Brace Jovanovich, 1979), by Betty Fairchild and Nancy Hayward. Its table of contents previewed chapters telling of gay families' stories—the parents' stories and the children's stories, examining what it means to be gay, what it's like being gay in the world, experiences of gay couples, the subject of religion and gays, families working together, and help available from support groups. These were all things I wanted to know about.

The second book was titled *A Family Matter: A Parent's Guide to Homosexuality* (McGraw Hill, 1977), written by Dr. Charles Silverstein. In the first half of his book, Dr. Silverstein had compiled stories of individual families and their struggles in coming to grips with having gay children. Maybe this would be a safe way for me to share experiences of other families without feeling exposed myself. The second half of the book dealt with medical and psychological issues concerning gays. Dr. Silverstein covered subjects like trying to get cured, masculinity and homosexuality, medicine and morality, and self-esteem therapy.

He had some things to offer that I hadn't thought of before.

I did find a third book on the shelf, but I decided to leave it. It outlined what parents could do to prevent their children from becoming gay. One of its main ideas was defining gender roles in children. I decided that was water under the bridge. I had to look ahead. I put it back.

I had my books—now all I had to do was check out. According to my definition of a secret—keeping a fact to oneself in order to hide the truth—my mind was entering the realm of secrecy. I had it all figured out: I could explain myself if my librarian friend started asking any questions. I would simply tell her I was doing research for a class of some kind. That made perfect sense. I also picked up an extra book, on an entirely different subject, just to throw her off.

I stood at the counter, waiting to see what would happen. I was almost disappointed when my acquaintance was totally oblivious to my reading material choices, not even seeming to care. She was more interested in a conversation she'd started with another staff person before I arrived at the counter. At any rate, getting through the process safely, just once, made looking forward to future visits much easier.

Over the next few months, I became much more informed and even felt free to share our secret with two or three close friends. With additional knowledge, I became more comfortable and my secret didn't seem so negative. I was able to add a few accepting and supportive friends to my small circle of confidants, and was on my way to a whole new world of ideas and experiences.

8

Releasing a Special Butterfly

Letting go of young adult children is probably one of the most difficult tasks parents have to master in the process of raising a family. We want to maintain control over their choices in order to protect them from real or imagined harm. We feel an obligation to guide them in directions that will prevent emotional wounding and physical injury. In the name of love and concern, we try to keep them wrapped in a safe cocoon under our care. It seems as if the more we insist on protecting them, the harder they struggle to break free. It's all part of a plan, a process necessary before we send them out to make their way in the world.

It was no different with Eric. We had made our way through his senior year just like any other year, but now May graduation was waiting around the corner, and it presented its own unique challenges and growing pains.

The day-to-day activities weren't much different than they'd been before—plays, musical concerts, prom and after-prom attended with Kirsten, as Amy had graduated and gone on to college. To the outside world, all was as it should be.

Eric did go to a few parties that we knew to be given by gay friends. We had committed ourselves to acceptance, so we tried not to say much. Still, we were uneasy, not really knowing what we were dealing with. We didn't talk about the parties much, but Eric did say he was finding that he didn't feel comfortable with all of the people he was meeting. We hoped that meant he was making good choices. He always had before, so we tried to remain optimistic.

Traci knew about her brother's homosexuality by this time. She, too, had found out by accident, during the summer before her junior year, at age sixteen. Her introduction to her brother's situation was not one he would have chosen for her.

She had found a letter from Ryan on Eric's desk. It was the first communication there had been from Ryan since the church conference in junior high. Thinking of him as a mutual friend, Traci had read the letter. Its contents gave her brother's secret away, and didn't leave the best of impressions. Ryan was living a fast lifestyle in a big city, and made no bones about it. Traci was caught totally off guard. She had heard kids at school talking about "faggots," and saying how gross and loathsome they were.

When she told Eric she'd seen the letter and asked him if he was gay, he'd had to tell her the truth he'd felt compelled to protect her from before. She'd thought she knew her brother. She didn't see him as being like the terrible stereotypes she'd heard about. She'd been close to Eric over the years, but this news left her feeling as if she'd lost her best friend. She was confused and scared.

She spent the night in her room in tears, not yet ready to accept her brother's offer to talk about it. We all knew then that we should have told her sooner what was going on. This was not the way for her to find out. We'd learned a hard lesson in family honesty and trust.

The passage of time—taking her turn at reading "the book" and finally talking to Eric—had helped Traci past some of her initial fears. Still, she felt somewhat betrayed. Why hadn't anyone told her? Being excluded from what had been going on in the family had put some distance between her and her brother. She was working through her own set of problems with the issue at hand.

I continued to read what I could find on homosexuality, and we all watched shows on television together about AIDS. We all wanted to know what was going on with that dreaded condition, known then as "the gay disease." We hoped the seriousness of this problem was having an impact on our son. He would be off to college in the fall, and we were concerned about what temptations might be presented.

Theater was the career Eric had decided to pursue, so that influenced his choice of a college. We wanted a liberal arts school with a broad base of courses so that he would be prepared with a back-up career if acting didn't work out. We looked at schools in the central United States, thinking of preserving the Midwestern values we had tried to instill in our children. Eric ended up enrolled in school in Dallas. He would leave in the fall.

I tried not to worry about the future, knowing I couldn't do much about it anyway, but occasionally I would wake up in the middle of the night in a panic. I had processed all I knew about the gay situation, but I still had trouble letting go of some of my fears about the unknown. When this would happen, I would get up and make my way in the dark to the overstuffed chair in our living room. There I would wrestle with my thoughts and concerns by myself, or with God in prayer. I would worry about whether we were really right to accept this thing as normal. I covered the same ground over and over. Were we making a mistake? Was it wrong? Was there any other choice? It was exhausting.

On one such night, I sat in my chair and thought about Eric, remembering what it had been like for the past eighteen years and thinking about how it was now.

As an infant he had been restless. I'd had to move him often and change his surroundings regularly. He'd had to be challenged. He was still like that—full of endless energy and always up for something new.

When he and Traci were preschoolers and they'd be ready to go somewhere ahead of schedule, we would play charades in the living room to keep them occupied and clean until it was time to leave. They would roll up in balls on the floor until I named an animal or a flower they liked, and then they would act it out. Eric loved to be a butterfly and Traci a flower. Eric had always teased and told me that it was my fault he wanted to be an actor.

Other than chronic poor handwriting reports, Eric's school conferences were always good. His teachers told us he was bright and cooperative, nice to have in class. They commented on his kindness to the other students. They recommended him for the gifted program. The positive reports continued in junior high and high school. We couldn't complain.

With all of this positive background, how could I think he was not OK? This new thing was just one small aspect of this son of mine. Maybe we had focused too much on the issue of sexuality.

I was tired of trying to sort out all of this. Maybe it wasn't up to me to understand—I didn't seem to be able to, anyway. There was just one solution. I bowed my head and prayed:

> *God, I'm exhausted. I don't understand this. There's no way of knowing what the answer is. All I can do is turn this whole thing over to you. I give you the homosexuality because you are the only one who knows for sure what that's all about. I thank you for Eric and I turn him over to you, too. You made him, and only you understand him fully. I know you love him, and so do I. I ask you to be with him as he goes out into the world. Help him to make wise and safe decisions. Thank you for being there for both of us, even when we aren't aware that you are. In Jesus' name, Amen.*

I felt a great sense of relief. I didn't have to understand. I'd done what I could, and now Eric was in God's care. All I had to do was love him.

I'd taken a writing class at our local college in the summer, and had found that putting my thoughts on paper was helpful. Now I turned on a light, found some paper and a pencil, and wrote.

Releasing a Special Butterfly

His fitful infancy
Made time in the playpen
Become a prison term;
He demanded to be freed.

Only minutes in the car seat
Caused him to cry out
Like a truck driver

Yearning to hit the road,
Bound for unknown destinations.

When he was four and waiting,
Again without the advantage of patience,
We played charades.

Our gold plush carpet turned to green pasture;
He became a butterfly,
His outstretched arms fluttered
Against imaginary wind:

He soared.

Mother wit
Put him in special classes,
Played with his thinking,
Gave him French.

Teachers
Sensed his kindness,
Lauded his maturity,
Questioned nothing.

In junior high, seasons changed.
He emerged from the cocoon of childhood
To attempt the free-flying patterns of adolescence.
He began to wonder if his colors were different,
Not from his lack of color vision,
But from a feeling in his heart—
Sometimes puzzling,
Sometimes wonderfully exciting.

Now he is nearly a man and seeking release,
Freedom to glide on newly seasoned wings
To break the stilted bonds of conformity,
Unknown, uncertain, unclear.

Spirit of my son and the butterfly,
I give him up to your care and protection,
Retaining only my love for him as I see him off
To daylight and darkness
Against the unsure sky of life.

9

Grazing

Letting go of things we can't understand or do anything about can be a freeing exercise. Sometimes we have to repeat that exercise several times before we are really rid of what is causing us frustration. It's like having a house with many rooms. One room is called the worry room. It's dark and cold for lack of windows to see through, or heat to remove the chill of despair. In this room is an old worn-out chair that sits low to the floor. When you sit in it, you sink down and the springs poke you. Whatever you are worrying about consumes your thoughts and keeps you tied to pain and discomfort. It makes it hard to get up.

The only way to get out of this binding grip is to make a decision to let go of what is weighing you down and get on with your life. If you can let go of the things that you can't understand or change, and trust that life is full of growth experiences—some pleasurable and some painful—it's much easier to cope. That process lifts you out of the depths and draws you into the light. Letting go of the worry and stepping through the door to freedom is great, in theory, but sometimes it takes several trips back and forth to the worry room before the process is completed. Each visit may be shorter than the last, as you go through the motions of letting the worry go, but eventually, freedom from despair can be accomplished.

As time went by and I learned more about homosexuality, I realized that things hadn't really changed that much in our lives. I was beginning to understand the process of learning to trust. The more things I let go, the less I worried. Eventually, I regained my confidence and was more at ease.

I didn't realize how much my attitude was changing until I received a magazine from a conservative religious organization we had supported for many years. The information they'd sent over time was family-oriented and Christianity-based. As I opened the pages of the mailing, I was expecting to see the usual subject matter on marriage and parenting typical of that publication. That wasn't what I got. What was printed on those pages hit me like a ton of bricks. The article I turned to was supported by the founder of the organization and was condemning homosexuality as a terrible sin. The copy indicated that this was a horrible phenomenon that we must treat with fear and disgust. According to the article, homosexuality was on the rise in our society and must be stopped. It was a threat to the very core of our morality. I was stunned.

As the shock began to wear off, I began to react. At first, I was hurt. This organization had published materials on child rearing and sex education that we had used in our home, with our children. I had trusted this organization and felt their support in attempting to give our offspring the tools they needed in order to be responsible, moral—and especially, Christian—adults. Now the head of this institution was indicating that my son was not OK—that he hadn't turned out according to plan, or that he was part of some kind of evil movement that must be stopped.

My emotions turned from hurt to anger. How dare he condemn my son! In a way, he had helped me raise Eric. I began to mutter and pace back and forth between my kitchen and family room. I would ask myself a question and then I would answer it. I've heard somewhere that you are headed for serious trouble when you start doing that, but I was the only company I had right then.

I finally realized that I had to stop. I was wearing a deep traffic pattern in my carpet, so I put a halt to my pacing. I had to do something, though. I couldn't just let this go without some kind of action on my part.

I rummaged through the desk drawer and found some paper and a pen. I'd write this character a letter. He'd given me his feelings about my son—now I was going to give him mine. He was going to get a second opinion, like it or not.

I started the letter by telling him how offended I was by the article—then I told him why. I said I had a son who was gay. I also listed what I considered to be Eric's finest character traits. I explained how he had lived his life thinking of others, helping with mission trips, and being involved in church activities. I told him that I hadn't seen any indication of immoral conduct from my son, and I didn't appreciate his condemning people he didn't even know. I let him know that we had used his ministry's materials in guiding our children, so if there was blame to lay, he might be ready to share it. In my final paragraph, I told him we no longer felt good about supporting a ministry that made blanket condemnations of entire groups of people. We wouldn't be sending any more money.

I'd written the letter so fast and so furiously that it was hard to read. I decided that it would be better typewritten. I typed it, put it in an envelope, and fired it off in the afternoon mail. I felt much better, but told myself that I would never hear back from them.

One afternoon about two weeks later, my phone rang.

"Mrs. Cole, this is the chaplain from...."

I was floored. I'd never expected anything like this.

"We received your letter, and we want you to know that we care about you and your family. This must be hard for you. Is there any way we can help?"

I'm sure I stuttered as I tried to respond to the man on the other end of the phone line. My emotions were bouncing all over the place. I was dumbfounded, touched, embarrassed, moved, and maybe even a little sheepish—all at the same time.

I managed to let him know we were doing OK and that I appreciated his call.

"We're sending you a copy of a book written by Barbara Johnson called *Where Does a Mother Go to Resign?* (Bethany House, 1979). She has a gay son, too. Maybe you'll find some help in what she has to say. We'll pray for your family."

I thanked him again and said I'd look forward to reading the book. After I hung up the phone, I headed straight to my mailbox. The book hadn't come yet, but I only had to wait a few days to get it.

Barbara Johnson has a compelling writing style. I was prepared for something interesting just from reading the clever title, and I wasn't disappointed. As my mind lifted the story from the pages before me, I began to understand where the title of her book had come from. She wrote about her four sons, who were special to her. Each had been a joy to her in his own unique way. In different ways, she'd lost three of them.

The first she lost to the war in Viet Nam. The second was killed in an automobile accident. The third had left home after she confronted him with information she believed linked him to homosexuality. To her it was a loss to sin and a separation from God. This loss was the hardest of all.

The pain in her story was clear, as she struggled with not knowing where her son was or what he was doing. She didn't know how he could be a Christian and be living the "homosexuality lifestyle." There was no guarantee that she would ever see him again. She was so depressed that she was afraid she might die. Even in her pain, a hint of the sense of humor she thought had gone out of her came through. She said she was in so much pain that her teeth itched. I found myself laughing one minute and in tears the next. Thank God Eric hadn't felt as if he had to leave home.

To her it seemed her son had made a *choice* to be gay. She couldn't understand why he would do something that seemed so against all he'd been taught. The counselor she went to backed up her fears by telling her that her son and other gays were suffering from paranoia. He told her about uncontrollable sexual desires that he saw as part of the homosexual condition. The way he saw it, they would just have to wait until their son was hurt badly enough to see the light and come home. Then he would be ready for "healing." This was hard for her, as he had been such a caring, sensitive son and she could hardly stand to think of him in that way. She couldn't imagine what had changed him.

Ms. Johnson was finally able to let go of some of her frustration through continued counseling, and by keeping a journal and praying. She felt the same isolation most families feel when they lack sources to turn to for answers and support. In her book, she spends a lot of time exploring the area of unconditional love—a trait that had always been a part of her faith. She turned her son over to God's care, as I had mine, thought of him only in terms of unconditional love, and prayed for him. She came to the conclusion that this was the only thing parents could do sometimes with their adult children.

As she dealt with her own frustrations, Barbara Johnson realized that there were others out in the world who were hurting as they dealt with homosexuality in their families—especially Christian families. She realized that there was something she could do to help others. For starters, she wrote the book about her personal experience and struggle. Then she established a ministry called "Spatula Ministries." This was a ministry to families who were "stuck to their ceiling" from hitting the roof when finding out they had gay children. Her newsletter, called *The Love-Line* was sent out to people who contacted her after reading her book. It was full of cartoons about life and parenting and faith. It featured letters from parents who wrote to her about their situations. It was a lifeline to many who were struggling and needed support.

I'd enjoyed the humor, courage, and compassion of this book's author. As a result of reading what Barbara Johnson wrote, I gave a lot of thought to how important unconditional love is in our lives and in our faith. I decided to pay more attention to that quality in my relationships. I agreed with her conviction that God is always there for us and willing to forgive, no matter what. Those promises were very important to my Christian faith.

There were a couple of major points established in the book that I felt uncomfortable with, however—possibly because of the other reading I'd been doing about homosexuality.

The two ideas I had the most trouble with were that homosexuality is a choice, and that it is a sin.

The facts given in the information I'd been reading seemed strong evidence that homosexuality is not a choice. The backgrounds of people who are gay vary greatly. Their experiences are different. Many have histories that are quite reputable, others don't. Even with these differences, all share strong, undeniable feelings and attractions toward the same sex, even when they fight those feelings with all the strength they have. Even with God's help, they aren't able to overcome those attractions. Psychiatrists can't help. Doctors can't help. Ministers can't help. How can it be that God would create so many people with such strong feelings, only to leave them stranded? It's not the God I know.

The second point had to do with whether or not homosexuality is a sin.

Most people who see it as a sin base their conclusion on scripture. Ms. Johnson indicated that this was the basis for her beliefs, too. How scripture is interpreted makes a big difference in the outcome. If passages are taken at face value only, the interpretation can be much different than if historical content and social customs of the times are considered. Literal interpretation concludes that homosexuality is a sin. More historical interpretation may come out a different way. I leaned more toward the latter. Because of that fact, I felt as if just "being" a homosexual was not a sin, especially when coupled with the concept of that orientation not being a choice.

At one time in my faith journey, I was more apt to look at the Bible in a more literal manner, reading every word and trying to figure out what I had to do to follow it to the letter of the law in my life. I felt great pressure to do the right thing, to always be perfect, to make the right decisions, and to stay in good standing with God. I found myself constantly dealing with guilt, and feeling I didn't measure up to the required standards I thought God had set for us. I was miserable. I had finally shared my frustrations with Jack, who was our minister at the time.

Jack had said to me, "Beverly, you have to decide if your God is a judgmental God who watches your every move and keeps records of your mistakes, or if he's a God of grace who gives you the freedom to make mistakes and be forgiven. Under which God can you function best as a Christian? In which mode can you best minister to other people? That's the bottom line."

I'd chosen the God of grace, because it took the focus off worrying about me and put it onto loving other people. I wasn't afraid of doing something wrong anymore. It was the most freeing advice I'd ever been given.

The insights on grace Jack had given me earlier in my life seemed to apply to this situation, too. That grace comes into play in relationships. How can we, as Christians, be the most loving in our relationships with homosexual people in our society? I needed another source of information.

In Morton Kelsey's book *Reaching* (Augsburg Fortress, 1994), the author talks about grazing like a cow in a pasture when you read. He says to take what is palatable and digestible and to leave the rest behind. That's what I'd done with Ms. Johnson's book. I'd benefited greatly from some of the things she said, but there were other things I needed to leave behind. I needed another Christian source of reading. I ran across *Is the Homosexual My Neighbor? Another Christian View* by Letha Scanzoni and Virginia Mollenkott (Harper San Francisco, 1978). It was time to go to another pasture.

Sometimes, in order to grow, we have to court change. The authors of *Is the Homosexual My Neighbor?* went beyond the common Christian concepts and ideas generally used as a basis for dealing with homosexuality. Some were within the confines of a safe comfort zone—familiar and easy to deal with. Others involved the risk of taking a look at new information. They even dared to give the view from the gay community's window.

The first concept that was dealt with was easy to swallow. We were asked to think about Jesus telling us to love our neighbor. The age-old commandment—to love your neighbor as yourself—was not a threatening idea. For centuries, committed Christians have tried to do that whenever possible, as part of their everyday living. The hard question came when it was suggested that the homosexual might be our neighbor, and that in order to love that person, we would have to get to know him or her better. We might have to visit with that person and find out what joys and sorrows are a part of his or her life. It could require us to go so far as establishing a friendship with one. It might even be advisable to do some reading to find out more about what it means to be gay. The book challenged readers to look at just how serious we are about loving our neighbors—all of them.

Another chapter suggested we look at where our moral feelings were really coming from in regard to gay people. Is it society—even church society—that is telling us gay people are on the bottom of the heap of sinners? Do we really feel that God would have us write off an entire group of people unless they conformed by repenting and changing their natures to live their lives as heterosexuals? Sometimes we have to look at the big picture and decide what God might really have in mind, even if it doesn't quite fit with what society says. The example given to make this point in the book was when God asked Peter to associate with Gentiles, a practice strictly prohibited by Jewish law. Had Peter stuck with what society said and ignored God, the Gentiles would never have heard the gospel or been a part of the church.

A third risk that might have to be taken in order to experience moral growth is that of putting compassion ahead of security. Most of us tend to choose action we know to be acceptable—the black-and-white action that no one will question. The problem with that form of decision making is that it gets in the way of compassion sometimes. It's safe to have compassion for the homeless or for someone who is sick, but there is too much controversy about homosexuality to risk getting involved in the suffering of gays in our society. There are many homes and outreach programs for teenagers who are in abusive living situations. There are few programs available for sons and daughters who have been kicked out of their homes because they are gay. There are all kinds of laws on the books concerning discrimination in housing practices against racial minorities and women. Unfortunately, if someone finds out that a person is gay and evicts him from his apartment because of it, there are no laws in most states to protect that gay tenant.

If we were free to care, no strings attached, we could be what Christ asked us to be. We really couldn't go wrong. Jesus certainly gave us food for thought when he said to us, "Truly, I say to you, as you did it *not* to one of the least of these, you did it *not* to me" (Matthew 25:45, italics added). To me, compassion is the way to go.

The Bible is used so often as a basis for condemning homosexuals. *Is the Homosexual My Neighbor?* deals with many of the verses used against gay people when the subject is being debated. I won't go into the details here, as that subject will be dealt with in a later chapter. I do feel, however, that it's important for us to look at a different scripture before we point out the faults of other human beings. Look at Romans 2:1. It tells us clearly that we have absolutely no right to judge others, and that when we do, we condemn ourselves.

In this book, *being* homosexual is looked at separately from *being* sinful. There is a call for a standard of ethics in moral behavior for all people, whether gay or straight. Heterosexual people need to be committed and responsible in their relationships. It should be no different for homosexuals.

There were many other tidbits to munch on in this pasture. Of interest was the chapter on what science is finding out, and how that has influenced our attitudes. There is also a chapter on what it might take for one to go from the mindset of homophobia to an attitude of understanding. Many other insights provided food for thought and valuable insight.

We form our opinions and make our decisions based on many types of information obtained from multiple sources. I believe that the diversity we experience in our search for answers on any subject is important. It adds value to those places where we find common ground. Sometimes it's hard work sorting out the flowers from the weeds, but I'm convinced that it's the only way to grow. We have to keep on grazing.

10

Sharing Lives

Domestic Violence Victims' Support Group, 9:00 to 10:30 a.m. Saturdays. Cardiac Support Group, 6:30 p.m. every second and fourth Thursday. Alzheimer's Support Group, 2:00 to 4:00 p.m. on the second Thursday of each month. Alcoholics, overeaters, widows, and the parents of all of the above—we have a group for you. I once saw a cartoon picturing a huge auditorium being used to host a convention. At the back of the room was a banner that read *Adult Children of Normal Parents, Annual Convention.* There were three people sitting in the otherwise empty auditorium.

Support groups—gatherings of people whose lives have been changed or at least affected by some event, circumstance, or condition. Strangers, sitting in a circle, pouring out their stories—failures and triumphs piled high in the middle of the room for all to see and evaluate. No thanks! Not me! I've always been able to solve my own problems in my own way. We all used to do that. When did this support-group craze start, and why has it become so popular?

I scanned the pages of the newspaper, amazed at the number and variety of support groups that had been formed to get people with common circumstances together. Head Injury Support Group. Parkinson's Disease Support Group. Compassionate Friends for those who had lost children. TOPS Club for those who wanted to lose weight. The list went on and on.

As I started to put the paper down, something caught my eye: Share and Care Support Group. Why did that ring a bell? I straightened the paper and followed the print with my finger...*for family members of gays or anyone whose family has been affected by AIDS. For information....*

Share and Care—I'd heard of it through a friend of a friend whose church hosted the meetings. When my friend first told me about it, I was surprised that there was such a group in existence, but dismissed it as something you turned to if you couldn't handle your problems on your own. That was reason enough for me not to join. I was just fine doing the reading I was finding on my own, and talking with a couple of close friends who provided free counseling as we took scheduled daily walks together. We'd shared everything over the years. We'd verbally raised our children together as we wore out pair after pair of sturdy walking shoes, beating the pavement for our physical and mental well being. They'd been wonderful, patient listeners over the last two years. I told myself I didn't really need extra support, but I couldn't resist reading the words again.

I was kind of curious about the other families who were dealing with having gay children, but the description also stated that the group was for people dealing with AIDS. That was a threatening idea for me. I didn't even want to think about that. What would I say to someone in that situation? I wouldn't have a clue. Besides, as long as I didn't know anyone who had personally dealt with it, the disease didn't seem real. I wasn't ready to get into that. I'd read enough. I put the paper away and decided to forget about the support group.

Putting it out of my mind should have been easy to do, but it wasn't. The idea kept eating at me as I went about my cleaning that afternoon. I'd wondered about knowing other parents of gay children when I'd first read about the support groups in Gloria Back's book, *Are You Still My Mother?* I was curious to know what we might have in common besides gay children. I knew, of course, that there would be differences, too. The AIDS issue was definitely uncomfortable for me, but it could happen in our family. You never know what the future holds. Maybe I could learn something. I still wasn't sure what I wanted to do.

My friend had given me the name of the lady whose church provided the room where the meetings were held. I'd written her phone number below her name on the scrap of paper I'd stuffed in the side pocket of my billfold. I decided to call her and see what she could tell me. Her name was Beth.

The phone rang twice before I heard the pleasant voice on the other end of the line.

"Hello."

I wasn't sure how to start, so I just jumped right in.

"Is this Beth?"

"Yes."

"Beth, I'm Beverly Cole. I was given this number to call if I was interested in the Share and Care Support Group. Do you know what I'm talking about?

"Yes, I do. What would you like to know?"

"I have a son named Eric, and he's gay." I was telling this to a total stranger.

"I have a son named Eric, and he, too, is gay," came from the other end of the line.

That was all it took. We had established common ground, and I was ready to relax and visit. We talked for almost an hour about our sons and our dealing with their being gay, what we'd conquered, and what we had yet to master. I was relieved that her son was not one of the ones with AIDS. I did ask her if that involved many in the group. She said about half of the group was affected. Some had sons who were sick, others had lost sons to the disease. There weren't any parents with lesbian daughters in the group at this time. They would be welcome if they wanted to come to the meetings, though. I told Beth my reservations about dealing with the AIDS families, and she seemed to understand.

"It's not something I like to talk about, either, but it is a fact of life. The group has helped me by providing current information. It's never easy to be involved in other people's pain, but it helps them so much to talk about it. Anyway, you are certainly welcome whenever you feel comfortable. You might find it beneficial, as I do, to go and talk, but mostly I find help in listening to the stories of the others in the group. It makes me count my blessings, if nothing else."

I copied down the next meeting time and decided to consider going. I had two weeks to make my decision.

Sunday afternoon, two o'clock—Dale came in from the garage.

"The meeting is at 2:30. Are you going with me?" I was getting nervous about actually doing it. I didn't have to go. I hadn't committed to anyone, but a part of me really wanted to go. I wasn't sure why.

"Can't. Have to work on my slide presentation. These Honduras trip slides are all messed up. They fell out of the slide tray when I dropped it after my last talk. I have to get them straightened up. My talk to the Optimist Club is at seven tomorrow morning." He held a slide up to the light, squinting to identify it. "You go ahead. You know how I am with that kind of stuff, anyway. I don't want to bare my soul in front of all those people—not my thing."

Dale is an outgoing person who never meets a stranger, but he doesn't like small groups where you talk about feelings and personal things in your life. He has always been one to just take things at face value and go on. He'd done that in accepting Eric's being gay. He was fine with it and didn't feel the need to talk to anyone about it. I knew all of this, but had hoped he'd go anyway.

"You go this time and see what it's about," he said. "Maybe I'll go next time, if you decide to go back."

It was 2:15, and I needed to get going if I was to be on time. I put on some lipstick, grabbed my car keys, and headed for the church. I tried to imagine how this would go.

"Hi, I'm Beverly and I'm a...." I'm a what? This is just a parent meeting with other parents. What's so difficult? It might be helpful.

Beth greeted me at the door with a smile and a name tag. As soon as she spoke I knew who she was. The remains of the Minnesota accent she'd brought with her when she moved to our part of the country gave her away. I'd enjoyed hearing it when we talked on the phone before. She was the one who had set the room up with a circle of chairs and a table to hold a pot of coffee and cookies brought by others in the group.

My hostess led me over to a long table where a tall blond lady was arranging books, magazines, and photocopied newspaper articles.

"This is another Beverly." Beth pointed back and forth from one of us to the other. "Beverly Cole, Beverly Barbo. Beverly Barbo, Beverly Cole." We laughed and said our hellos.

"You're welcome to take any of the duplicated articles on the table and to browse through the rest." The resource person made a sweeping hand motion over the table.

"Where do you want these books?" A slightly graying man appeared in the doorway carrying a box that was obviously heavy.

"On the floor next to the table would be fine, Honey." Beverly Barbo turned to me. "Beverly, this is my husband, Dave. Dave, Beverly."

For the next ten minutes, an interesting assortment of people assembled in the room. The room that had been just another Sunday school classroom earlier in the day now served as a different kind of gathering place. Some people hugged each other, while others held back, waiting to be introduced. Most looked to be at least in their forties, as I was—far enough along in life to have sons who knew their sexual orientation.

One couple was of particular interest to me. I noticed them right away when they entered the room. The husband paid close attention to his wife, never letting go of her hand. She was attractive, with an especially creamy complexion that was marred only by the dark circles under her eyes. I wondered if the young woman who was with them was their daughter. A fragile quality shared by the two women gave a clue that they were somehow related. The husband made an attempt at conversation when he introduced himself and the others to Beverly. The only person I could hear him indentify was an older lady who was the fourth member of their party. He introduced her as their minister. I assumed we would find out what that was about later.

The other Beverly called the group to order. "I think everyone is here. Would you please find a seat?"

She started the meeting by giving a report about what was going on around the country with the gay community, personally and politically. As she talked, it became obvious that she and Dave were not only group leaders, but also advocates for gay rights. She said that gay and lesbian adults she had met across the country were in a great deal of pain because so many of their parents had kicked them out—declared them dead. She shared what it was like to march in gay pride parades next to these rejected young people, trying to affirm them as worthy human beings when their families would not.

"There's such love and caring among those walking down the street, arms linked in unity for a common cause, for justice for our gay citizens. There's such healing for those who have lost their families by rejection, and for those of us who have lost our children by disease." She talked about the struggle that was going on in the political arena, attempting to get the Reagan administration to take the AIDS crisis seriously. More research was desperately needed, but because it was thought to be a gay issue it was being put on the back burner.

"It falls on deaf ears and is dealt with by clay feet." her voice was angry.

After the opening informational comments, the personal sharing began. Dave and Beverly's story was one of deep sorrow and regret. It had only been a few years since they had lost their gay son, Tim, to AIDS. The impact of his death on their lives was apparent, and they struggled to keep control of their emotions as they spoke.

They talked about the struggle Tim had gone through, growing up in a small town. It had been obvious from early on that their son was different, "one of the gentle people," his mother said. "He just didn't fit in, somehow. We loved him with everything we had to give, but it wasn't enough." The intensity of her voice raised as she went on. "The scars from childhood teasing and rejection followed him into his adult life and had a profound effect on him. The other kids were ruthless in their name-calling—*faggot, queer, sissy, girl.* He knew intimately the cruelty that insensitive children sometimes heap on the heads of those who are different, weighing them down with harmful emotional baggage, making their lives miserable. It sabotaged his self-esteem."

When he left home, it was to move to San Francisco. His mom said that his new life was like that of a kid in a candy store. Finally, there was a place where he fit in, where he was loved and accepted as he was. Nothing was out of his reach. Unfortunately, during this time in his life, he was caught up in the fast lane and made some unwise decisions. It may have been then that he'd contracted AIDS. It eventually robbed him of his prime and yanked him away from family and friends and from his loving partner, Tom.

"We were with him as much as we could be, from the time he was diagnosed until he died," Dave added. He drew circles slowly on the piece of paper that lay on the desktop in front of him. "Beverly actually lived with Tom and Tim the last six months of Tim's life."

After their son's death, Dave and Beverly felt that they couldn't just sit still and do nothing. Beverly wrote a book, *The Walking Wounded* (Carlsons', 1987), telling their story and giving information to educate people about homosexuality in families and about AIDS. She and Dave were active, traveling all over the United States, going to meetings and becoming informed in whatever ways they could. Beverly gave talks to any group who would listen—churches, clubs, college groups—attempting to help people understand, and trying to love and lend support to the gay community in the process. They admitted that it was a hectic schedule, but they were committed.

The combination of their knowledge and experiences had undoubtedly been a helpful source of information for the group. I'd already gathered a pile of articles from the resource table and was realizing how little I knew about what was happening across the country.

Ruby and Howard were the next to share. Their son, Larry, was born in 1950. He had dated girls all through high school, but his mother had known since his junior high years that he was gay. "In a small town, it was just easier for him to date girls than to try to explain."

"Eventually," Howard said, "I knew, too."

Together this couple had decided to love and accept their son as best they could. They'd known of other gays who weren't so lucky. Other parents had thrown their children out when they'd learned of their orientation. Ruby shook her head as if she couldn't believe this.

"There was no way we were going to do something like that to our son." Ruby's voice faltered. "In 1986 Larry called us from his home in Colorado and said he had the flu. We didn't think much about it then, but things snowballed. He kept getting sick—flu, pneumonia, and then—the final diagnosis—AIDS. In 1988, at the age of 37, Larry died. We lost our son."

Ruby had made a quilt block for Larry, as a part of the AIDS quilt project. She described it as having a pale blue background with a picture of Larry and a photo of the flowers from his funeral on it. There was a dove and a copy of a poem entitled "High Flight" worked in, too. She said that making the quilt block in Larry's memory had been helpful to her and her husband in their mourning process. Their son would always be remembered that way. It was quiet in the room for a moment. Ruby looked at Ruth, who sat to her left. Ruth knew it was her turn to speak. Her voice was quiet but strong.

"Willard and I were raised with a strong religious faith—Mennonite. That faith is shared by our son, John, who completed a full course in seminary and served as a pastor for four years."

Ruth's story was about what had happened after John answered the call to the Christian ministry. He'd felt confident enough of that call to commit his life to it. While in seminary, after years of private struggle, he admitted to himself and his family that he was gay. That realization brought spiritual peace, but vocational uncertainty.

John went to a faculty counselor for support. He didn't know if he should—or even could—continue on his planned course. The counselor affirmed John's acceptance of his sexuality and his gifts for the ministry. So John decided, after some agonizing, to enter the pastorate and just stay in the closet.

Ruth and Willard exchanged glances, sharing the weary energy of those who must repeatedly testify to hard truths. "Staying in the closet worked for a while," Ruth continued, "but eventually, John found that to be impossible. A small study group at the university Christian fellowship he pastored was sharing individual spiritual pilgrimages. John realized that his struggle with being gay had profoundly deepened his love for God. So he took the risk and told the whole truth. The small group kept the information confidential. But simultaneously, a heated debate about sexuality was taking place in our denomination. This led to controversy, first in the fellowship and then in the conference, over John's position on homosexuality. John realized that he must come out of the closet fully. As a result, he lost not only his assignment with the fellowship, but his license and opportunity for ordination, as well."

Ruth took a deep breath, fingering the handkerchief she grasped in one hand. The pause seemed to be Willard's cue to continue.

"It was painful for John, our family, and the fellowship John served so well. He ultimately felt he'd been forced to turn God down on his life's calling." Willard couldn't hide the disappointment in his voice. "We've tried not to be bitter, but it's hard sometimes. John has a good job as an administrative assistant now, and is an active layperson in an accepting congregation. He's doing OK, but it's such a loss for those he could have served from the pulpit."

Ruth nodded in agreement, mirroring Willard's expression of quiet pride.

I was next to tell my story. It didn't seem like much of a concern, after hearing the others. I almost felt like I should pass to the next person. My story was relatively uneventful compared to the others we'd heard. Eric was well and happy and working on an education that would lead to a career he'd been interested in since he could talk. Acting was a profession in which being gay was fairly well accepted. Our family was doing OK. We hadn't had much real trauma to deal with. Most of the sons we'd heard about so far were older. Maybe that factor had put them more at risk for getting AIDS.

"I guess the AIDS issue scares me a little," I shared with the group. "It's something we haven't been affected by personally. I realize now that it's real. What can I do about it?"

Beverly came to my rescue.

"Like you, many people don't realize how real it is until it's too late. That's what I'm trying to address as I speak to groups across the country. Young adults don't always sit and twiddle their thumbs as we would like to think they do. Many are sexually active, and it isn't just fun and games anymore. It can be fatal. We can't bury our heads in the sand. Safe sex is a must. It's a must for kids who are straight as well as for those who are gay. AIDS is not just a gay disease, as some would have us believe."

Our leader shifted from talking in general terms to speaking in a more personal way. "Tim explored for a time, after he first left home. As I said before, that's probably when he contracted the virus. Later he met his partner, Tom, whom he loved very much. They had several wonderful years together. They bought a house and were making a life with each other. We loved Tom like one of our own. The boys liked so many of the same things and shared a strong religious faith. Unfortunately, it was too late. Tim had found that special relationship after he was already infected. That's why we need to educate people early. Beverly, there is additional information on the resource table if you want to look into it more."

I hadn't picked up any of the AIDS materials from the table before, but I would take another look before I left. I hoped there was something I could send Eric.

Beth sat on my left and was ready to speak. She, too, felt fortunate to have a son who was in good health, had a good job and was leading a happy and productive life. There was a bonus in her situation—her Eric had a loving partner who had been part of his life for several years.

" I don't know what Eric would do without him."

Eric was her son by her first marriage. His father had died, and Beth eventually remarried. Her second husband was supportive and accepting of Eric and his gay orientation. She was grateful for that.

"Eric isn't hard to like. I may be a bit partial, though." She laughed along with the others around the circle. "People have always commented to me on how kind and considerate he is. Sometimes, when they point that out, I tell them he's gay. Most people are surprised, but not critical—at least not to my face. I figure it kind of opens their eyes when someone they know and seem to respect turns out to be gay. It can't hurt. Hopefully, it makes them stop and think."

She told a story about a family funeral they had attended years before. The weather was cloudy, but no one had been too concerned about the threat of showers. When it came time to go to the cemetery, the sky opened up and there was a downpour. Eric had thought ahead and was waiting at the door of the funeral home, his arms loaded with umbrellas. That was typical for him, according to his mother.

"He's had good luck as far as discrimination goes. When he was in intensive care recovering from a heart attack, the hospital staff treated his partner like immediate family. There was no trouble with visits. That isn't usually how it goes with gay partners. They aren't always allowed in."

Beth had wanted to give something back—to help those less fortunate. She had helped to train volunteers at the Crisis Hotline in handling calls concerning matters of sexuality. "You would be surprised at how many there are. I suppose suicide calls are what we get most. Kids get rejected, kicked out by their families, and are devastated. Sometimes they are just tired of being called names. Here is some information on the Hotline." She handed me a stack of brochures to pass around the circle.

As a Christian, Beth did have one regret concerning Eric. He had pulled away from the organized church. The condemnation of gays by the church didn't fit what he felt Christianity was supposed to stand for. It was unfortunate, but not uncommon. She had done her best to convince him that not every Christian felt that way, but he had not had many experiences that showed him otherwise. She tried to understand his viewpoint, but it was still a disappointment.

The family who had brought their minister with them was the last to speak before break time. The young woman with them was their daughter. Their story was especially tragic. They had found out that their son was gay and that he had AIDS at the same time. What a blow.

"We really didn't have time to think. The son we'd raised had come home to his family, and he was dying. There was nothing else to do but love him and take care of him. That doesn't mean it was any picnic, but we did what we could to let him know he was loved. I guess we're trying to deal with the rest of it now that he's gone." She blinked hard, but it didn't stop the tears.

I hadn't been introduced to this woman, and I couldn't see her name tag, but my heart went out to her as she spoke, whoever she was.

Her husband continued. "Our minister has been great." He glanced at the older lady who had come with them to the meeting. "I don't know what we would have done without her. No one in our community has said anything. We don't know how much anybody knows. It's really been stressful."

Their minister was sitting between the mother and the daughter and was holding hands with both of them. It was obvious that they were hurting. I suspected it hadn't been too long since they'd lost their loved one.

I was glad for the break. We'd been sitting for quite a while, and part of the sharing had been overwhelming. I wasn't sorry I'd come, but a glass of tea and a brownie were a welcome distraction. Chocolate relieves stress in any circle. I picked up more reading material and visited with some of the others in the group before it was time to resume.

I hadn't met all of those who were left to talk, but I could see their name tags. Lucille would be first, then Marcene, and finally Gene and Jeannie.

I should have been forewarned of what was to come, as Lucille let out a long sigh of hesitation before she began talking. As the pieces of her life fit together to form her story, I vowed never to complain about problems in my life again.

Lucille told us about her son, Steve, who had accepted his homosexuality when he was a sophomore in high school, but hadn't shared that information with her right away. It wasn't until twelve years later, at the funeral of Lucille's mother, that the fact was revealed to her.

"We were in the car going home after Mother's service, when I asked Steve if there were any women in his life. He gave me a puzzled look and said, 'Mom, don't you know I'm gay?' I was floored. For some reason, he thought I'd figured that out, but I hadn't. Unfortunately, he had to go right back to New York, where he was living, so we didn't have a lot of time to discuss it. My husband was gone by this time, so I couldn't even discuss it with him. In a way, that was a relief. I don't think he would have understood."

Her story was a series of crises, one piled on top of another. Seven weeks after her mother's funeral and her son telling her he was gay, her sister called to tell her their father was full of cancer.

"I remember saying, 'God, this is too much at one time. I'll deal with what I can and I'll lay the rest aside.' That's what I had to do until a year later when Steve called and told me he'd been diagnosed with AIDS. It was like a huge wrecking ball had been dropped on me and I had to pick it up and run with it." She shifted in her chair.

Lucille was a school teacher and had limited vacation time, but whenever she could, she had flown to New York to be with her dying son. He didn't want to come home to die. She was relieved in a way, as the AIDS care in her small-town hospital would have been limited. He was better off in a hospital where staff had experience with the disease and he would have friends nearby. She hadn't been able to be with him when he died. She was notified too late that the end was near.

When it was over, she felt that she had to talk to someone. She took a chance on a priest from the Episcopal church in her area. His help had proved invaluable. He helped her to work out her grief by getting involved in things. He got her started working on the AIDS Task Force. Eventually, she was assigned to the task force that was active in her wider church district. She'd been helping there ever since.

Marcene's son was David. She'd known he was gay since 1974 when he was nineteen. He had graduated from their small-town high school and had gone to college for a couple of years. He eventually moved to San Francisco, where he made his living bartending and working as a waiter in different hotels. He was happy, and for thirteen years all was well.

"Knowing David was gay, when my husband and I started hearing about AIDS we were naturally fearful. Even though it had been in the back of our minds since 1982, it was still a horrible shock when he told us in '87 that he was infected. He wanted to come home to live and be with his family. He did move home for the last six months before his death. We were fortunate to have a caring, accepting physician and a wonderful hospital staff. I don't know what we'd have done if they'd given us any trouble. I kept a journal, kind of a log, during David's illness. It's a record of our schedule, his symptoms, and how he was feeling day by day. Maybe I'll do something with it sometime, but I'm not sure what."

Marcene described the quilt block they'd made for David. "Its background was made from a blue tablecloth trimmed in green leaves. Our daughter, Debra, and I designed the cranberry lettering that was used to name the places he'd worked and the people who had been special to him. Howard and Debra's girls, Holly and Tanna, helped us to sew the lettering onto the panel. Then, each person in our family signed it and added a personal message to David in the bottom set of leaves."

After David was gone, Marcene had felt the need to do what she could to prevent this tragedy from happening to other families. She put her own grief aside and served on an AIDS awareness panel, giving information at local schools, civic organizations, and speaking anyplace people would listen. She also trained for the PWA—People with AIDS—program. The volunteers made themselves available to AIDS patients for whatever service was needed. "It didn't involve much actual medical care. Mostly it was just a matter of being there and loving the patient and his family."

She told us about Paul, whom she'd cared for for nearly a year before his death. With his cousin's help, she'd made a quilt block for her friend.

Then there was John, whom she'd been with for only eight months. After he died, she took the sketches he'd made her and designed a block for him.

The third young man was only under her care for three months, but he, too, had left an empty space in her heart.

"It's hard. I have to take time off in between cases. It takes a lot out of me, but it's something I want to do."

It was getting late, but time had gone quickly. The last couple was ready to share.

Gene and Jeannie were small-town people, just like many of the others. Gene's hair was white, Jeannie's just beginning to gray. They'd driven for two hours to come to the meeting. They hadn't been in the group long, but they told us how grateful they were to have it available to them. It had been a lifesaver for them.

After their son, Kelly, had been on his own for a while and living away from their small community, he told them he was gay and that Ron, his roommate, was really a boyfriend, a partner. It had been a shock, and had taken a great deal of effort on their part to adjust to the news, but they were learning to accept things the way they were. The threat of death hung heavy over their family also, but it didn't involve AIDS. Their case was tragically unique in that they were dealing with the possibility of suicide.

"Kelly admires people who are proud they're gay." His dad spoke first. "He feels that people should accept others just the way they are. Because of this, he has a hard time staying in the closet, where he might not be so vulnerable. He can't seem to do this. The staff at the hospital where he works found out he was gay and made his life miserable. He even lost one job because of it."

Jeannie added her comments. "When things go wrong, he's devastated and calls home in the middle of the night, threatening to take his own life. It keeps us in a constant state of panic. We're always terrified of the final phone call that might tell us he's followed through. There's no one in our small town to talk to. We feel so alone. It's affecting my health. Sometimes I don't know if I can take any more."

Jeannie was shaking. Beverly took her hand and suggested that individuals send cards of support and encouragement to Kelly.

Jeannie took a deep breath and let go of Beverly's hand to dig in her purse for the small black book that held his address. We each copied it down.

It was nearly five o'clock. It had been an exhausting yet helpful afternoon, but I was ready when Beverly suggested we break up for now. No one left immediately. There seemed to be a need to wind down before going back to our everyday lives—kind of a re-entry from outer space after being somewhere foreign for a while.

Share and Care—I guess that's really what we'd done. In the beginning I'd hesitated, clinging to my own need to be strong and independent—to do it myself. Now, I realized that it wasn't only about me and whether or not I was strong enough to take care of my own problems. It was about all of us sharing our strengths, our weaknesses, our courage, and our vulnerability. I thought about the attitudes of the group members when they first came into the room at the beginning of the afternoon. They had been tentative, serious, reserved.

As I visited with people afterward, their burdens seemed lighter. They were smiling and standing up straighter and somehow taller. We had an obligation to each other to give what we could and take what we needed. I suppose the needs would change from meeting to meeting, depending on who was a part of the group and what was happening in their lives. I knew one thing for sure now: when I looked at the support-group page of the newspaper, I would have new respect for what that term really meant. People's tragedies are real, and we need to stick together to support each other. It had been my experience in the past that things happen for a reason, and we end up in places we never expect to be. I prayed that I would never have to come to this group for support in dealing with AIDS in our family. Maybe coming and picking up information would prevent that. At any rate, I would be back with Dale, another time, sharing lives.

11

Crossing Bridges

When you have a son or daughter who longs to be an actor and who says starvation is not a problem, it makes you wonder. Most parents are used to thinking in terms of financial security for themselves and their grown children. When people talk about a career in acting, they use words prefixed with *un,* like unsure, unsteady, unpredictable, unstable, and unwise. All of that makes the parents of budding young actors uneasy. We had all of the apprehensions that accompany this whole scenario as our son entered the world of theater. It was like sending him across a bridge over the Royal Gorge without any handrails.

On the other side of the coin, however, was the influence of friends who, like us, were beginning that dreaded state in life known as middle age. Some were looking back and having regrets. We'd heard stories from friends who'd chosen the path of financial security at the exclusion of pursuing some wonderful, fanciful dream of youth. They'd fed their bodies, but denied their souls.

With all of the data in for consideration, we'd decided to give our blessing to Eric, encouraging him to follow his bliss—to go for it—theater or bust. Interestingly enough, eventually that "go west, young man, and follow your dream" spirit landed him right in the middle of northwestern Nebraska—the part of the country first settled by our brave pioneers.

After his first year in college, Eric decided to audition for summer stock theater. He tried out for several programs and was accepted into one offered by the Ft. Robinson Post Playhouse Theater Company, a small group connected with the Ft. Robinson Resort near Crawford, Nebraska. It might just as well have been Broadway, though, since it was Eric's first professional acting job and an opportunity to show what he had as an actor—and he'd be surviving on his own financially. He was excited, and so were we.

We were pleased for the obvious reasons, but there was more to the story. Ft. Robinson held a special place in our family's history. It's an old cavalry remount station that has been preserved by the state and converted to a tourist attraction, a place where families can come and have a good time together. We had taken advantage of that facility when our kids were in grade school and had wonderful memories of our time there. We'd enjoyed crafts, horseback riding, jeep rides into the scenic buttes—and above all, plays at the Post Theater.

Eric's employment at the Ft. Robinson Post Playhouse was somehow symbolic. He had come as a child to see plays that had sparked his interest in acting and now, as a young adult, he was going to be acting in those productions. It was kind of an initiation from childhood into adulthood.

We couldn't pass up the opportunity to revisit this memorable spot and see our son perform in his first professional acting roles. It would be fun to see how his acting skills had developed with a year of college training. We invited my parents to join us, and they volunteered their recreational motor home for the trip. We packed up a week's worth of grub, fired up the horsepower, and rolled our wagon west.

When we finally arrived, we inquired as to where the actors were living and then set out to find the building where Eric was spending his summer. It was easy to find, and so was Eric. He was standing at his front door waiting for our arrival, grinning like a Cheshire cat. I'd figured he would be glad to see us, but I was surprised to see how glad. He was glowing all over and almost giddy. I thought this acting life must be agreeing with him. I was loving his enthusiastic and affectionate greeting, but in the back of my mind there was a quick bleep from my "mother radar" mechanism. I didn't know why. I decided to dismiss it and just enjoy the moment. Time would tell if there was something more to it.

The next hour or so was spent touring the living quarters that Eric shared with the rest of the cast and getting reacquainted with the small theater where he and his summer company poured their hearts out for each evening's performance while the sweat poured down their backs in the un-air-conditioned facilities. We met several other members of the summer company and were pleased to see how well they all seemed to get along with each other.

Finally, we let Eric go so he could take care of some back-stage duties and we went back to the camper to rest.

Time for the evening performance came quickly, and we were excited. The weather was hot and muggy, so we stood outside the theater for as long as we thought we dared without losing our chance for good seats inside the limited-capacity building. There was a nice-looking young man who was greeting people and welcoming them to the Post Theater. We hadn't met him during the day, but he was obviously with the company. Finally, it was our turn to be greeted.

"Hi, I'm Craig. I'm the stage manager. Welcome to Ft. Robinson." He was tall and slender, with sandy-colored hair. His eyes were bright and they lit up with his smile. I couldn't tell what color they were in the dim light, but they were friendly, as he was. He had an innocence about him, like John Boy of "The Waltons" television show, which was popular at that time.

We introduced ourselves and my parents, and listened to what else he had to say.

"It's so good to meet you. Eric has been excited about your coming, and I've been looking forward to getting acquainted with his family. Did you have a good trip?"

We continued to visit until it was time to go in and get seated.

"Enjoy the show." Craig flashed his compelling smile once more and left us to choose our seats inside the theater.

Eric was the piano man in the show, and the rest of the cast filled the parts of other characters typical in a melodrama. The actors played their parts well, and we laughed until we had tears running down our cheeks. It must have been fun to have such a good time and to entertain others in the process.

It was late when the show was over, and Eric had to stay to help take down the set so that a different one could be put up for the next day's production. We set a time for him to join us at the motor home for a home-cooked meal the following noon, and we all called it a day.

The next day Eric came over to the campground for lunch, as planned. Dale and my dad had gone to find a part they needed to fix something that was broken on the camper, and my mom had volunteered to fix lunch. Eric and I were free to talk. We talked about the show we'd seen and about who each of the actors was. He told me general things, such as where they'd gone to school and where they were originally from. He also told me that almost half of the group was gay or lesbian. I was surprised that there were so many.

"Shelly was the short girl with dark hair," he went on, "Jason was the guy who played the villain. Craig was the stage manager you met before the show. Did I mention Shelly?"

As he reviewed the names of those in the cast, my radar kicked on again and my mother's intuition was activated. I sensed that I was on to something. Maybe it was a shade of difference in Eric's tone of voice. I took a chance.

"Craig is someone special, isn't he?"

Eric looked at me with a crooked grin and nodded his head.

I remember thinking, *This is it—what you've wondered about—the moment of truth. There's another live person in the picture here, and there's no turning back. Here's another young man who is obviously gay, too, and Eric cares about him. It isn't kid stuff anymore. It's one man having a relationship with another man, and you're about to find out what that's all about—ready or not.*

Either Eric knew I needed more information or the silence was driving him crazy, but he started filling me in.

"Craig is twenty-three and just graduated from college this spring. We hit it off right away. We do everything together. I help him with whatever I can for the stage managing and he helps me with my stuff. On our days off, we go sightseeing. We go up to Mount Rushmore and explore caves and hike. We have picnics and go to the movies, and just have a good time. He's a great guy, and it's so much fun for us to be together. It's so cool, because we can hold hands and be who we are, and it's no big deal. There are other gay and lesbian couples here, and straight ones too, and it's fine. He's been anxious to meet you guys. I hope you can get to know each other a little better while you're here."

The only response I was able to get out before the men got back and my mom called for lunch was, "He seemed very nice when we met him last night."

Maybe we would have a chance to finish our talk later, but for now we needed to get some of Grandma's fresh green beans into our starving actor.

We'd come here to enjoy what Ft. Robinson and the Post Playhouse had to offer, and to check on our son's theatrical progress. All of that was essentially the same. What had changed, however, was our focus: where before it had been on the individual dramatic productions, now it was on the half hour before each evening's production when we spent time with Craig. He made his nightly rounds, greeting visitors and promoting good public relations as his job required, but his biggest P.R. job was with Eric's family. He did it well. We found him to be very likable, charming, easy to talk with, and sincere. We could understand completely why Eric had been attracted by this young man's charm and wit. Craig's enthusiasm was contagious. What was not to like?

The summer season ended, and Eric was home for a few days before he went back to school. He had mixed feelings about his summer being over, but he was anxious to return to school and friends. Craig's picture sat on the desk in his room. Eric said he missed him terribly.

His eyes would fill with tears and he'd complain, "I don't know when I'll see him again." It was obvious that their relationship was very important to him and that there was a big void now that they couldn't be together. I was beginning to understand that a caring relationship is a caring relationship, period. Seeing real people and sincere feelings involved was starting to make a difference in my skeptical attitude. My heart went out to Eric and Craig. I could see that parting was difficult in any close relationship, gay or straight.

Eric's time at Ft. Robinson had been life-changing. When he met Craig, he crossed the bridge from being a gay boy, wondering what that mystery was about, to being a gay man, understanding the joys of a caring relationship with another human being.

When Dale and I met Craig, we'd liked him immediately. That person and his relationship with our son was a source of comfort and helped us take another step toward acceptance. We went from a stage of apprehension and fear to one of understanding and confidence. We had crossed a bridge, too. We felt good about Eric's choice of a relationship and about the way he seemed to have in mind to live his life.

Eric's grandparents were even affected by Craig's charm and by how happy Eric seemed to be in the relationship. They'd known for some time that the grandson they loved was gay, and they were trying to understand from a perspective two generations away. This was a step toward that understanding.

What the future held for Eric and Craig remained to be seen. They would have to cross that bridge when they got to it.

12

More Bridges

It was fall of 1988. Eric had been back at college for about a week when our phone rang one evening. He was talking so fast it was hard to understand him. He tended to do that when he was excited about something.

"Guess what! Craig's coming to Dallas. He's going to try to find a job teaching or stage managing so we can be together. Can you believe it?" He took a breath and chuckled. "Couldn't live without me, you know. That's going to be so cool. It's going to be a great year."

Eric's prediction was right. His sophomore year in college began with good times and great companionship. When we would call to talk to Eric, his roommates would tell us that Craig and Eric were out for ice cream or at the opera or buying groceries to cook dinner.

With each other for company, they explored the big city. On one occasion, when we did make phone connections, Eric told us about the gay western night club they'd found.

"You haven't seen anything until you've walked into a gay western night club where guys are dancing with other guys and they all have on Texas-sized cowboy hats. That was a strange sight even to us."

It was a good feeling to know that Eric was happy. We all want our adult children to be in caring relationships. You just never expect it to be with a person of the same sex.

Just before Thanksgiving, Eric and Craig had an opportunity to do some entertaining together. Traci, by then a freshman at another college, had called her brother to see if she and a friend could come spend a few days before the holiday. Eric's break was shorter than his sister's because he was involved in a campus production of *Godspell*. She had it all figured out when she called.

"We have a ride all arranged to get to Dallas. Then, maybe I could ride back to Mom and Dad's with you. Laurie has her arrangements figured out, too. What do you think?"

"That'd be great, Trace. You guys can come and see the show, and then we can all do Dallas."

After a year and a half, Traci was feeling better about her brother being gay. She missed him and was looking forward to her visit.

Eric and Craig were perfect hosts. Just as Eric had promised, they "did" Dallas. On the first night, the girls had the best seats in the house for *Godspell*. Traci and Laurie stayed afterwards to help strike set. Taking down scenery, a mundane job if you are a theater major, was a treat for the girls. Later, they all had a late supper at the Black-eyed Pea, one of the guys' favorite restaurants. The next day, the foursome went to Six Flags over Texas for their grand finale. For three starving college students and one starving assistant stage manager, Dallas was "done."

Eric and Traci arrived home together, ready for their holiday break from studies. I could tell when they walked in the door laughing and harassing each other that the relationship was getting back to normal. Traci had taken her camera to Dallas, and had two envelopes of photographs to show for it. Thanks to a one-hour film developer, she had a record of her first college road trip.

"This is one of my favorites, Mom." She held up a picture of all four of them at the amusement park—arms linked and everyone laughing. "I feel a lot better about all of this gay stuff. Craig is so nice, and we all had a great time together. Eric's really happy. I still don't understand it all, but I know now it's going to be OK." It seemed she, like the rest of us, was beginning to be able to live with this unusual twist that was going to be part of our lives forever.

Eric must have sensed that we were getting a little more comfortable with his situation. The exact level of that comfort was tested when he asked me if Craig could come to spend some time with our family at Christmas. I told him I'd have to talk to his dad and would get back to him.

Eric seemed pleased when I told him it would be fine for Craig to come. "We'll look forward to it. He can stay in the extra bedroom in the basement." We would look forward to the visit, but I wanted the ground rules to be perfectly clear ahead of time. "OK?"

"Sure, Mom. That's cool."

It was a week before Christmas, and Eric and Traci were due home as soon as their finals were over. I was working on a grocery list when the phone rang.

"Hi, Mom."

"Hi, Eric. You sound kind of down—tired from your finals?"

"No, it's something else. I thought I should let you know. Craig isn't coming home with me."

I was afraid to ask. "Everything OK?"

"No, things haven't been going very well between Craig and me lately. We're probably going to break it off. We're going to go our separate ways for the holidays and see what we think after that. Maybe we've just been spending too much time together."

"Are you OK?"

"Yeah, it's pretty much mutual. We'll see. I'll be home in a few days."

"That's fine. See you soon. Drive carefully."

Christmas of 1988 came and went. The months following it were rocky in terms of the relationship between Eric and Craig. They made several attempts to make it work but finally gave up. They parted ways with a shaky friendship at best.

In August of the following year, Eric and Craig saw each other by way of a mutual friend in Dallas. Craig had spent the summer working in Galveston, and Eric had gone to summer school in St. Louis in preparation for changing schools. He'd gone back to Dallas to visit friends before he started the fall semester, and that was when he saw Craig. They found that time had healed their wounds, and they enjoyed seeing each other again—the time had come for them to be friends again.

Craig told Eric that he was on his way north to spend some time with his family. He was looking forward to the visit, but dreading the long drive home. Eric offered to check with us about providing an overnight stop to break up Craig's trip. We were surprised to get the call, but glad to help. It wasn't unusual for our kids to send weary travelers our way. Sometimes I had wondered if there was an invisible "motel" sign over our front door. At any rate, we marked the date on our calendar and looked forward to seeing Craig again.

It was late when Craig arrived at our house, two weeks to the day from Eric's phone call. He'd been on the road for twelve hours and was a tired traveler when he pulled into our driveway. We agreed that a visit would be more enjoyable over breakfast and after a good night's sleep.

"Are you anxious to see your family?" I asked, sipping my hot tea at 7:00 a.m.

"I really am." He buttered a bran muffin. "It's been a while. I miss being able to get together with them. My stage managing jobs seem to tie me down, even on the holidays. I don't get back as often as I'd like. There are twelve kids in my family, plus my parents. Kind of hard to get everyone there at the same time."

We talked for a while and finally I felt comfortable asking a question I'd been wondering about.

"Craig, I hope you don't mind my asking you this. Just say so if you do. I wondered if your family knows about your being gay?"

"No, I don't mind talking about it. They don't know. I would like to be able to tell them about it. I think it's great for Eric that you guys know. When my folks were in Texas to visit, it would have been nice if I'd been able to tell them the truth about Eric and what he meant to me. You want to be able to share stuff like that. They're pretty conservative, though. It might really hurt them. I'd never do that."

After breakfast, I walked him to his car. He reached in the door and picked up a couple of framed pictures of his family. "This is a picture of all twelve kids and my parents. I'm number eleven."

He identified his brothers and sisters by name and told me a little about each one. The other photo was of his parents alone.

"They're good people. Maybe someday I can tell them who I am. I don't know."

I gave him the names of two of the books that had helped our family when we first learned about Eric. One was *Is the Homosexual My Neighbor?* the other was *Are You Still My Mother?* "They would both be good books to have in hand if you ever decide to tell them."

He thanked me for the bed and breakfast and was on his way.

Several years later, Dale and I were in Costa Rica on an eye-care mission trip. When we got back, we checked our phone messages and found one from Craig.

"Hi, Coles. This is Craig. I just wanted to tell you I did it! I told my parents and they took it well. I couldn't find both books you recommended, but I did go prepared with one. I'm so relieved. They said they would read it and try to understand. Thank you for your help. 'Bye for now."

I felt a great sense of relief. I was pleased with Craig's parents' response. He deserved their love and acceptance, and it sounded as if he might be getting it.

As I look back, I realize what a difference a person like Craig can have in one family's life.

Eric, through his relationship with Craig, had experienced the exhilaration of first love and the pain of that love ending. Now, it seemed that they were going to be able to have a friendship. We, too, felt a friendship toward Craig. I hoped we'd be able to stay in touch in years to come.

For Traci, Craig had helped to bridge the gap that could have formed between brother and sister. She had been able to see someone she liked and was comfortable with next to her brother. She felt better about a part of his life she'd been having trouble understanding before.

Even Craig had been able to cross a bridge by revealing to his parents who he was and what it means to love each other in families—no matter what. Perhaps by providing moral support, we had been able to give him back something of what he'd given us.

I guess events in our lives, not unlike events in a theater career, sometimes feel like crossing the Royal Gorge on a bridge without handrails. Hopefully, the love of family and a love for other people we meet along the way are available handrails to grab onto, to keep us from losing our balance and plunging into the jagged depths below.

13

My Funny Valentine

Being different and living in a society that doesn't always understand differences is difficult. Sometimes even the love and support of friends, family, and lover isn't enough. So it was with Kelly.

One cold winter evening Gene and Jeanne, a couple we'd met at the support group, came to our house for soup and to visit. Dale and I hadn't known their son, Kelly, but we'd known his parents for several years. On this particular day Dale had seen them as patients during the day and then they'd come over to our house for supper. We spent the evening talking to Gene and Jeanne about Kelly. By the end of the evening we knew his story and we wished we'd known him.

"Kelly loved being a clown," his parents told us, and the story unfolded from there. He'd put his makeup on carefully, paying close attention to every detail. His greasepaint smile set the stage for an afternoon of cheer for nursing home residents. The crow's feet around his eyes accented the winks he shot across the room to coax giggles from kids having lunch at McDonald's. Mothers had to remind their delighted children of their obligation to the Big Mac and fries on the table in front of them.

Kelly's costumes were covered with stripes or polka dots, or maybe even a touch of paisley to accent the exaggerated movements and gestures he'd learned in clown school. He loved being able to combine what he had learned in classes with his own natural ability to bring out the best in older people and children, to make them happy, to help them forget their troubles. He understood the need for a moment or two of escape from the real world once in awhile. Kelly had not had an easy time growing up.

The day Kelly was born to Gene and Jeannie was a day set aside on everyone's calendar for love—a good omen, his parents thought. It was Valentine's Day, 1965. His older sister Kim was thrilled to have a new baby brother to love and help care for. His early years were happy until he went to school.

Kids seem to have radar when it comes to zeroing in on another child's weak spots. Kelly was an extremely sensitive child, and his classmates soon picked up on this. They discovered that if they teased and made fun of Kelly long enough, they could upset him and make him cry.

This sensitivity would prove to be a double-edged sword as Kelly's life story unfolded. That quality, along with a high-strung personality, caused the school authorities to recommend him for special education classes by the time he'd reached his freshman year in high school. He rode the bus to classes available in a larger town nearby. He really didn't have any problems with learning, but they thought he might have emotional problems. Kelly's family wasn't very happy about the recommendation, but agreed to try it.

Kelly ended up tutoring some of the other students in the class. This was his first opportunity to see the good that giving of himself could do. He began to realize that he had talent and a natural compassion for people. Almost daily he found ways to show concern for them.

One of the stories his mom told us about was his paper route. The newspaper in any town as small as the one Kelly was raised in is an important link to the larger outside world. Kelly delivered this paper to many of the citizens in his community. The news wasn't all that he delivered, however. Many of Kelly's customers were elderly folks, and whenever he didn't return home in a reasonable amount of time, his mother didn't worry. "I figured he'd gone back to somebody's house with the tractor to clean snow out of their driveway— someone who couldn't do it themselves or he'd gone to run a few errands for them. He didn't charge them. He just enjoyed helping out."

His natural rapport with the elderly led him to take a nurse's aid course. He and his mom took it together, and both worked in nursing homes in nearby towns. The patients loved him, and often asked for him specifically. He seemed to understand their needs.

Sundays were spent singing in choir and candle-lighting at the church he and his family attended.

One task Kelly's family enjoyed was keeping up a small local cemetery. They would all go out together to mow the grass, trim around the headstones, and keep trash picked up. On hot days, they would take a break for a cool drink and to rest. Kelly had a favorite spot for their breaks, near a heart-shaped headstone. He said he wanted one like it when he died, since his birthday was on Valentine's Day. His mother would nod and finish her drink without comment. That would be up to someone else. She would be gone by then.

After high school graduation and vo-tech school, Kelly decided to leave his small farming community to see the world. He got a job in a city many times larger than his hometown, in a nursing home. It seemed that Kelly was on his way to a happy adult life.

One weekend, Kelly was home for a football game. He sat with his parents and the minister of their church. His mom thought he seemed edgy, and noticed that he had even been drinking some. She knew that something was bothering him, but she had no idea what it could be. Finally, he asked her to walk with him to the concession stand. That walk would change her life. Kelly told his mother that he had been struggling for a long time with something he felt he had to share with her. She couldn't imagine what might have him so uptight until he said the words.

"Mom, I'm gay." He explained as best he could how he'd come to this conclusion. He also told her that Ron, his roommate, was in fact his partner—more than just a friend.

Jeannie was in total shock. She asked him all the questions parents ask when that bomb is dropped. "Are you sure? What did I do wrong? Where do we go from here?"

Kelly's mother couldn't sit through the rest of the game. She made her way to the car and just sat there in a state of shock and in tears. She was overwhelmed with feelings of guilt and shame. She relived Kelly's entire childhood over and over, trying to remember what she had done that might give her a clue to the cause of this horrible affliction.

Their minister drove Kelly home and his numb mother went home with her husband.

Jeannie remembered feeling very alone. "You just don't talk to people in a small town about something like this." Her minister had been of some moral support, but he really couldn't understand what she was going through.

She decided to attempt to go on with her normal activities, trying to hide the pain she was feeling. That proved to be just what she needed to do.

Jeannie went with a carload of friends to a hospice meeting as part of a training program she was enrolled in. The speaker was Beverly Barbo, who told the story of losing her gay son to AIDS. She offered her book, *The Walking Wounded,* as a help to anyone dealing with terminal illness.

Jeannie couldn't believe it. It was an answer to prayer. Here was someone to talk to who would understand her problem. But how in the world was she going to get a chance to see Beverly Barbo in private? The ladies Jeannie had come with were ready to go and in a hurry. Jeannie's mind was racing. Aha! A deposit slip from her checkbook would work. She scribbled a quick message, giving as much information as she could in the limited space she had available. She handed it to Ms. Barbo without a word, only a quick glance. The guest speaker scanned the note and responded, "I'll call you."

When the call came, it was as if a huge burden was lifted from Jeannie's shoulders. They talked for an hour, and Jeannie poured her heart out. Beverly kept assuring her that it was *not* her fault. She told her about a support group for parents of gay children. Gene and Jeannie started driving the two hours it took to get to the city where the meetings were held.

"The timing was perfect, Gene told us. "We all needed some kind of support. Kelly was having trouble on the job." It wasn't the first time. In the hospital where he'd first worked, he told his superiors that he was gay. He admired gay people who were confident and proud of who they were. He wanted to be proud, too. His superiors didn't see things that way, and they started causing him trouble. Kelly was giving patients the compassionate care he was so good at, but it didn't matter. He lost his job. Besides this, a close relative made his life miserable whenever he would go home for a visit. This person would call Kelly horrible names and tell him what a disgusting person he was.

With all of this going on in his life, Kelly would get discouraged and call his parents in the middle of the night to threaten suicide. Jeannie would talk to him for hours, trying to get him settled down. She would hang up the phone in terror, not knowing for sure if she had convinced him to survive. The support group sent Kelly cards of support to try to keep him going.

Kelly got his EMT certification and started driving the ambulance for the hospital. The improvement of his qualifications seemed to have been a good step for him. Things should have been better in his life, but they weren't.

He went to the office to pick up his check one evening, and the staff told him not to come back the next day. They had filled his position. They had been on his case since the beginning. When questioned later by the personnel director who had hired him, the staff said they were afraid of Kelly because he was gay.

He couldn't understand why they wouldn't just accept him for who he was. He did his job responsibly. He had finally come to grips with being gay, and it wasn't interfering with his job performance. Why was it so hard for them?

This was the last straw for Kelly. He couldn't take it any longer. While his partner, Ron, and another friend were out one evening, Kelly stuffed rags under the garage door and started the car. He closed his eyes and took a deep breath. In a few minutes he was gone. His life ended at twenty-five. The irony of it all was that Kelly loved cars, and with the help of this one he finally got relief.

"Ron had to call us to let them know that it was over. Kelly was at peace at last. There would be no more phone calls in the middle of the night." Jeannie's voice faltered.

The note said, "It isn't your fault, Mom. I love you all."

I remembered Kelly's funeral as his parents reviewed it with me.

The service was perfect, down to the last detail. Ron, Kelly's partner, was a set and costume designer in the civic theater in the city where they'd lived together. Ron saw to it that Kelly looked just right, especially the details of his hair and the EMT uniform. He touched up the makeup to cover the burn left on Kelly's forehead from the car exhaust pipe in their garage.

Some of us from the support group had attended the funeral and were pleased to see a large showing of townspeople, relatives and friends who came to remember Kelly and support his family.

"Kelly has his heart-shaped headstone now, and every June 22nd, the anniversary of his death, we receive a flower arrangement from Ron and a note saying how much he misses Kelly." Jeanne told us with tears in her eyes.

"Hearts and flowers are symbols of love and acceptance. That's all that Kelly really wanted."

Kelly is not the only gay person who ever committed suicide. It's thought that one out of three suicides is committed over issues of sexuality. Kelly had his family's support, but not all gays do. Some families completely disown their gay children, saying that they have brought shame on the family and are no longer welcome in their homes. Many families even go so far as to tell their gay children that as far as they are concerned, the child is dead. Society, in general, doesn't understand or accept gay people as normal or as people of worth. Some religious groups call gays an abomination. That image isn't very good for one's self-esteem. Many gays experience discrimination on the job as well as other places, just like Kelly did. Many employers don't think of equal opportunity as including homosexuals. There are no laws in most states to help them. Hopefully, Kelly's story will raise awareness so that his life won't have been lost in vain.

As for now, Kelly, rest in peace. You are loved.

14

God Is in This Place

Minneapolis, Minnesota, was a place Dale and I had long thought would be beautiful to visit in the winter. We had a picture in our minds of the entire landscape smothered in a blanket of clean, white snow. We imagined leafless trees and evergreens trimmed and decorated with the pure white art of nature. We envisioned children and adults alike practicing their figure skating drills on ice-covered ponds that sparkled in the great northern sunshine.

In February of 1991, we found that dream coming true when Dale found a professional meeting in Minneapolis. We were excited about seeing firsthand what the travel brochures could only show on paper.

We were not disappointed. Everything we had imagined about this part of the country was true—and more. Besides the breathtaking beauty of nature, there was splendor in the big city skyline of downtown Minneapolis. The architecture showed a marked contrast between the old and historical and the new and artistic.

The downtown shopping area, called Nicolett Mall, was made up of several city blocks of buildings that housed stores ranging from Pier 1 Imports to Saks Fifth Avenue. These groups of stores were connected by a network of covered walkways that made the shopping area fit together like a carefully woven web spun by the cleverest of spiders.

Most of Dale's daytime hours were spent in professional education classes, so I was on my own to entertain myself until evening. I found myself overdosing on the availability of interesting shopping for three days straight. Suffering from eyestrain and credit card exhaustion, I decided to spend Saturday afternoon just exploring the area around the hotel.

The change of scenery was refreshing. I shared the snow-covered paths of Loring Park with bushy-tailed gray squirrels, busy with their day's work. I enjoyed watching parents and their young children circling the frozen pond on ice skates, busy with their day's play.

The outdoor sculpture garden across from the Guthrie Theater fascinated me as I wandered in and out among wooden animal forms, ceramic people shapes, ancient mythological creatures, and profound social statements in bronze. I made a mental note to share it with Dale before we left the city.

The afternoon was slipping away, so I retraced my tracks through the park, said good-bye to the squirrels, and headed back in the direction of the hotel.

I had chosen Grant Street to make my way back. Just as I prepared to turn on Nicollet Mall Street to end my afternoon adventure, something further down Grant caught my eye. It was a beautiful old historical Methodist church, Wesley Methodist. I had noticed it when we came in on Thursday. I decided to walk by it before I went back to the hotel.

I looked for the main entrance, hoping that there might be worship service hours posted. I did have Sunday morning free, and it might be fun to attend their services. I found the door I was looking for—and something I wasn't looking for. On the side of the building was a plaque stating that Wesley Methodist Church was a reconciling congregation. I couldn't believe it. I had read about reconciling congregations, but hadn't encountered one until now. I felt a chill go down my spine. Reconciling churches openly welcomed gays and lesbians to be a part of their church. They were all welcomed with unconditional love and acceptance. I couldn't believe what I was seeing. It was the type of church I had hoped Eric might someday be a part of.

I almost ran back to the hotel. I could hardly wait to tell Dale. We were going to church here on Sunday. We were going to see what this was all about.

Sunday morning it was freezing cold outside. We walked briskly down the two blocks to the church. Inside the church doors we were met with warmth that soon overtook the cold we'd passed through outdoors. We were greeted and ushered into a church that shone as if the Murphy's Oil Soap cleaning crew had been there. The restored sanctuary was framed in beautiful cherry wood and was filled with historic church charm.

We sat down and began to take in our surroundings. We looked around the congregation to see an average membership age of about sixty-five. There were young families seated here and there, contrasting the differences in ages. I couldn't help but look to see if there were any same-sex couples sitting anywhere in the pews. I saw a few. A single man caught my eye as he came in alone. He was thin and had patchy hair. He walked with a cane. I wondered if he had AIDS.

There was a mixture of races and income levels. There were people there in fur, and some in denim. I knew already that this was going to be an interesting experience.

We looked at our bulletins to see what else we could learn. There were classes offered in dealing with hate crimes. There was an AIDS support group. There were projects set up to feed the poor and homeless.

A lady we had met at the convention had come to church with us. She pointed out to me what interesting programs were offered to this congregation.

I felt that it would make things clearer for her if I explained reconciling congregations. When I told her that this church had made a group decision to openly welcome gay and lesbian people unconditionally into their church family, she frowned. I thought she was going to disapprove. Instead, she made a very profound statement.

"It's a church. Why should they have to *decide* to welcome someone? I thought everyone was supposed to be welcome in a church."

She had made a good point.

The service started and the choir sang the Introit. I found myself trying to figure out which people in the choir might be gay. Had I not learned anything from my reading about trying to stereotype gays and lesbians? I was ashamed of myself.

The lay leader came to the podium to present the concerns and make announcements. She said their minister was at an area conference where a vote had been taken concerning removal of language degrading to homosexuals from Methodist church policies and publications. The conference had voted seventeen to four in favor of removing it. The congregation clapped and cheered. There were many people sitting in the pews around me who were old enough to be my grandparents. They were so open-minded and loving. I could hardly keep the tears back.

When the collection plate came around, I made my monetary gift, but also left a note of thanks on a little scrap of paper. I thanked them for being such a loving congregation, and wished them well in their continued effort to serve all of God's people.

As we walked out among the rich, the poor, blacks and whites, the young and the old, gays and straights, I couldn't help but think, *God is in this place. Thanks be to God.*

Minneapolis, Minnesota, had shared many kinds of beauty with us—some not promoted in the brochures.

15

Prayers

Spring is a time when families should be outside, cashing in on the perks of the season—sunshine, blue skies, and daffodils pushing their yellow heads through the soil to meet with the warmth lingering in the April air. On this particular Saturday afternoon, we would not be affected by the epidemic of spring fever that was running rampant on Traci's college campus. Instead, the three of us would put our outside activities aside to participate in an event being held within the walls of the old campus fieldhouse—the public display of the Names Project AIDS Quilt.

My memories of the fieldhouse took me back to my own college days when our highly ranked Big Eight basketball team had attracted sellout crowds whose enthusiasm filled the air with noise and electricity, as well as filling every available seat in the house. Hot, crowded, and deafening—that about summed it up. I remembered what all of that had been like, but I had no idea what to expect from this event.

As we crossed the street from the parking lot to the sidewalk in front of the fieldhouse, I scanned the pavement from one end of the block to the other. I wondered if Fred Phelps, the well-known "Minister of Hate," would be making an appearance, accompanied by his band of followers. This so-called man of God was notorious for showing up at the funerals of people who had died of AIDS, and at places where the AIDS quilt was being displayed. He made no bones about hating gays, and took whatever opportunities he could to demonstrate against them with signs reading "God hates fags" and "Gays are going to Hell." He made no distinction between the AIDS funerals of gay and straight victims. To him, AIDS was God's punishment wherever it reared its ugly head. I was relieved to find him absent from the pavement surrounding the building. It was too nice a day to be spoiled by bigotry.

We entered the building through the main entrance, ending up in the area that had held concession stands and restrooms in times past. There were tables set up for the sale of T-shirts, buttons, and posters—all promoting the Names Project and AIDS research. On the floor next to the table was a plastic bucket that held many colors of unarranged carnations that could be purchased for a donation. "Remember a loved one," the sign next to the bucket read.

Music that was barely audible beckoned us through the doors and into the old gymnasium. Where there once had been deafening crowds, there was now a near-deafening silence. It was like a huge tomb. At first I felt as if we were intruding, but soon I got caught up in the atmosphere where we would share these families' most personal moments, remembering those who had been dear to them. Now, those precious loved ones were only memories stitched together in squares and lying on a gymnasium floor. I had a strong sense of God's presence as I observed from the entryway.

The larger quilt was made up of twenty squares laid in rows—five squares long and four squares wide. These were set apart by long strips of contrasting cloth to divide the blocks, much like a real quilt. Inside each of the twenty squares were housed thirty-two rectangles measuring six feet by nine feet. I thought of a conversation I'd had with Beverly Barbo about the quilt, and of how beautifully she had put into words the symbolic meaning of the quilt.

"The three-by-six foot panels are approximately the size of a casket. Gravestones, not chiseled from stone but made from cloth by loving hands." It had sent chills down my spine when she said it. She could speak from experience, as she had made squares for her son, Tim, and his partner, Tom—both gone now, taken away from their families by AIDS.

At first I just stood in the doorway and looked out over the entire quilt in all its colorful splendor. It was a blend of color, like a Monet painting. It was also a blend of lifetimes shared by many families made one by similar tragedies. It was a common prayer, pleading with God and man to remember their children.

I made my way over to the outside edge of the quilt. I knew when I began to view the squares one by one that the two hours we had allowed would only be enough to begin covering the stories to be told by the fabric that was laid out on the floor in front of my feet.

The first was a red rectangle decorated with gold letters that spelled "Eddy." There was no last name.

"There is a lot of shame that goes with this disease," Beverly had told me. "It's not only the disease, but being connected with the gay issue that is hard for families who haven't come to terms with it. It isn't just a gay disease, though. AIDS has taken the lives of many people in many situations. At any rate, some families won't use last names or let others making blocks for their loved one use them either."

I prayed that this man's family would someday accept him honestly and remember him as he was—all of him.

Next to the red fabric was a white piece. In one corner was a photo of a nice looking, middle-aged man in a military uniform. His full name was written in red script across the white background. There were military patches, ribbons, and insignias filling the corner opposite the photo. I thought to myself, *He made it through the battles, but he lost the war.*

There was a blue piece with an enlarged photo of a man named David. Beside the photo of his face was a felt heart that served as a background to frame the things that had been important to him in his life—his business card, a wine label, an Oreo cookie label, and pictures of his cocker spaniel puppy. The dates of his birth and death were under his name. He died at age thirty-two. The size of the photo made a statement. It said that David and his friends were proud of who he was. They were not ashamed to show his face, that he might be counted worthy of recognition.

Lord, be with those who were proud of David.

Children, too, can fall victim to the ruthless AIDS virus. One panel looked as if it had been made by a young child. The pale background was framed in purple, and at the bottom was a crudely painted row of grass and flowers—red flowers. *Cory* was the name painted in huge purple letters across the sky. The dates were 1983-1987. Cory's life was a short one, but the words to the song "You Are My Sunshine," printed inside a bright yellow sun, told the story of the effect that young man had had on his family. I mourned and wondered what he might have been if he'd had a chance to grow up. I know that his mother must wonder, too. I imagined she might have been one of the mothers Beverly had talked about, who had a hard time giving up the block made for her child.

"It isn't that uncommon," Beverly had told me. "Some hang onto their blocks for months before letting go. Others make duplicate blocks so they won't have to."

My prayer was for peace of mind and acceptance, whatever the circumstances surrounding her beloved child's death. *Blessings to all who were left behind to mourn that little life.*

There was one block that was just a plain rectangle with huge block letters stating the loved one's name. Simple. The underlying message was, *Remember this person; I do, and I loved him enough to make this block with his name on it.*

The design itself reminded me of a documentary I saw about the quilt. It was called "Common Threads." One of the stories told in the film was of a gay couple who loved each other very much. They both ended up infected with AIDS. The first man taken ill was loved and cared for by his partner until the day he died. The second partner decided he wanted to remember his lover and friend, so he made him a quilt block. Before he died, he also made his own. The designs were simple, plain backgrounds filled with huge block letters stating their names. Appropriately, the blocks had been stitched together in the same group of eight.

Thank you, God, that they found love in their lives.

Beverly had told me of mothers and sons who sat together while the sons were still alive, working on the blocks. I couldn't imagine doing that, but I could see how it might be helpful in working through the grieving process ahead of time and together. You would always know that the design pleased the one it honored. It would still be painful.

A block remembering a man named Steve brought to mind another comment Beverly had made to me when we'd talked about the quilt.

"One of the hardest things about being involved in the justice issue of homosexuality and AIDS is that as you go back time after time to view the quilt in different places and at different times, you have unpleasant surprises. Tim had a wonderful friend named Steve, who was kind of a soul mate, a spiritual buddy. They loved to get together and discuss their faith, talking openly about their relationships with Jesus. Steve was the one who did Tim's memorial service. It was one of those rare and precious friendships that comes once in a lifetime. Some time later we wrote to Steve, but hadn't heard back. We were puzzled as to why he hadn't responded. Later, as I scanned a new section of the quilt in a different city, I knew. Steve was no longer on this earth. He was again with Tim, in a better place."

Thank you for the beautiful human beings who make life good because of who and what they are to us in our lifetimes.

A square that had *I love you, Daddy* written in huge handwriting brought to mind a question I had asked Beverly: "Are most of those remembered on the quilt gay?"

"In the past," she told me, "the percentage of AIDS victims who were gay was high. According to a *Time* article, 'The Changing Faces of AIDS,' that percentage is shifting. The number of gays testing HIV-positive is lower, and the number of heterosexual men, women, and children is increasing." Her voice had shown a tone of urgency at this point in the conversation. "When these HIV cases become full blown AIDS in the next few years, we'll have a different picture. The general public will be shocked. That's why it's so important to educate everyone."

It had been difficult, but I'd managed to stay in control of my emotions on this Saturday afternoon, as I viewed the memorials stretched out across the gymnasium floor. I could only imagine what the lives of the people represented there had been like, and who their families were. But so far I hadn't had to get too close—not until now.

As I rounded the corner of one of the large blocks, my eyes fell on a royal blue memorial that changed the level of my participation. There, on the rich background was centered a multicolored rainbow with a picture of Tim Barbo on one end and a picture of his friend and partner, Tom, on the other. This was real, and I had to find one of the many boxes of tissues that had been placed along the quilt edges for those who might need them during the viewing. I was now one of those people.

Underneath the photos of Tim and Tom were their full names, birth and death dates, and the words—"Together Again in a Better Place." There were pictures of family and friends and the letters used in Tim's memorial service. A letter from Beverly reviewed all of the wonderful memories that had been part of Tim's growing up. In it, she mused about some of the boyhood mischief he'd been into as a part of the process of growing up. She wrote to him about the family's love for him, and of their admiration for the way he'd lived his life. The words celebrated his courage in health and in sickness. Who he was as a person was affirmed loud and clear by Tim's mother. Beverly had let it be known that her son was in a better place now, and that brought them all peace.

There was a letter from Tim to Tom, written for one of their anniversaries, telling him how much he loved him and how he felt the love of Christ radiating from their relationship.

This square wasn't just cloth, glue, string, and sequins. It was life and death, love and family, and we knew the people involved. We knew their story. We knew their grief. We felt their loss, and this made it all too real. As I stood beside Tim and Tom's square, I soaked tissue after tissue as I prayed.

> *God of the Barbos and the Coles and all of these other families, thank you for these lives—some still in full swing, others tragically over and done with. I know that you love each of the people remembered on the cloth spread at my feet. Why is it so hard for society to accept something different? Why do there have to be illnesses like AIDS that are so devastating and so hard to figure out? Whatever the answer, Lord, I don't think for a minute that you are punishing anyone. I'm glad you are available to your people in these hard times. I'm grateful for the caring that individuals have shown in the lives of those who have been ill and died. Although I don't believe you send tragedy on us, I do think we can learn from it. Be with young people and nudge them in their decision making about drug use and matters of sexuality. It really can be fatal. Be with health care workers who are responsible for blood supplies. Above all, God, I thank you that you hear our prayers and are with us, no matter what. In Jesus' name, Amen.*

By now, Dale had joined me beside the blue memorial and Traci was beside him, tissues in hand and eye make-up smeared under her eyes.

"I didn't think it would be this hard." Her empathetic nature couldn't be denied. It was one of her best traits, as far as I was concerned.

We left the display feeling mixed emotions. We certainly felt the tragedy of the lives lost. Most of these people were in the prime of their lives. What a waste of love, life, and talent. Who knows what any one of these people might have contributed to society. We'd seen squares for doctors, lawyers, athletes, and many others. We'd seen squares for the kind of people who live right next door to us, who mow their grass and tend their gardens.

The other side of the coin was more positive. Everyone represented in the quilt that covered the gymnasium floor was loved by someone. That was evident in the memorial stitched together in his or her name by families, friends, or people with whom they had been very close. These people had not died in vain, as this huge work of art had made their deaths more visible. It called attention to the urgency of the need for AIDS research to find effective treatment and finally a cure. The progress had been slow before, but the quilt was raising awareness and beginning to get results.

Beverly and I had talked at length about what we as parents could do to affect this crazy thing that had made such an impact on our society. What Beverly said made a lot of sense.

"As parents of gay children, we have to try to accept them as they are and let them know they are good people. We have to teach them self-esteem. If we don't start teaching our gay children that although they may be a little different, they aren't bad, we are doing them great harm. Let them know that God does love them just the way they are, and so do we.

"There are teen programs available," she continued, "that help them learn where they can go to meet other gays—places that are safe and acceptable. There are wonderful resources available through the PFLAG organization."

She'd talked about how we have to teach our gay and straight kids values and responsibility in relationships. Gay kids often buy into society's stereotype of the fast, irresponsible lifestyle, thinking of that as the only option. We teach our straight kids values, and the same ones apply to the gay kids.

I'd laughed when she said this, because it brought to mind a conversation I'd had with Eric several years before. I'd told him that I accepted his homosexuality, but I wanted it to be clear that I wouldn't be very happy if I thought he was sleeping with every Tom, Dick, and Harry. Then we'd both laughed because that used to be something you would say to your daughter. Before it came up in conversation, I'd never thought about how it would apply to a gay son as well as a straight daughter. Values are values, and they apply across the board—and appropriate decisions need to be made accordingly.

Beverly had continued with her observations. "Once families get past the point of thinking that it's their fault or the fault of someone who has been a bad influence, or that their child is somehow getting back at them for something, then progress toward acceptance can be made. It's hard for families, but the sooner that can be accomplished, the better. Drug and alcohol use and suicide attempts are so often the result of parental and societal rejection. Hopefully, early acceptance and understanding can help them to avoid some of those snares."

I agreed with Beverly entirely when she said, "We need for our kids to know that they have just as much right and just as great a possibility for having a special person in their life as our straight children do. Committed relationships are not out of their reach. Maybe someday those unions will be more accepted by society, and it will be easier."

At the center of each display of the AIDS quilt is the signature square, a 12 foot by 12 foot expanse of blank fabric where visitors to the quilt are invited to kneel on the square and leave their own memorial message or mark. I didn't leave one when we viewed the quilt, but if I had, this is what I would have written:

My prayer is that someday soon this epidemic will be a thing of the past and we can fold up the quilt and put it away. The lives lost in its unfortunate membership can be laid to rest—their contributions to medical, social, and political justice made. Amen.

16

Extinguishing the Light

It's amazing how fast a single event can negate a good mood— even ruin an entire day. One minute you're on top of the world. The next minute, you hit rock bottom. An uplifting event that has sent your spirit soaring on wings of joy can be followed by another that brings it crashing down, splattering it all over the ground. Dale and I experienced a day filled with this wide range of emotions in the fall of 1992.

Traci was involved with the rowing team, the crew, of a large state university. In this sport, little training is done directly on the water in the fall and winter months. Most of the conditioning and skill-building is done on rowing machines called ergometers. Instead of having rowing regattas on state lakes and rivers, competitive events are held inside on the ergs. On this particular Sunday afternoon, some members of the university's team had traveled to the state capitol to participate in one of these competitions.

Dale and I had gone to the meet and had enjoyed an afternoon of cheering for various members of the crew we'd gotten acquainted with over the previous months. We might have been accused of being a little extra enthusiastic when Traci did her event, but we did try to support everyone equally, as best we could.

In an erg race, the participant races against time and endurance while sliding back and forth on a wooden seat, using strong legs to propel his or her body to and fro. At the same time, the athlete is pulling and releasing a rope in an opposing motion, using upper body strength. It's an event that requires power, coordination, and endurance.

Traci had been working hard to improve the number of strokes per minute needed to complete the timed exercise. Her second-place ranking, along with a twenty-two second improvement on the time from her previous meet, was cause to celebrate. Excitement ran high for her personally, for us as parents, and for the rest of the team who were there for support. Many other members of the team placed well that day, too, so spirits were high. We hated to see this peak day come to an end, but it did, in spite of our wishes. We gave Traci the

83

old athletic "high-five" and left for the two-hour trip home.

The main street of the capitol city is a beautiful, tree-lined, well-landscaped avenue. That afternoon the sun was shining through the trees, giving the street an aesthetically pleasing, almost nurturing effect. Children playing in the public park that was centrally located on the same street added to our visual enjoyment.

Unfortunately, what was taking place around the perimeter of that public park was not aesthetically pleasing or nurturing. It was quite the opposite.

I was oblivious to our surroundings as I dug in my purse for a pair of sunglasses and wondered what one wears to the Olympics. Dale startled me as his voice broke through my daydreaming.

"Bev, look at this. I can't believe it."

There on the sidewalk, walking in two different directions along the edge of the park, were about twenty demonstrators with protest signs. I guessed the ages of those participating to range from five or six to fifty-something. They were standing together in groups of two or three. They were conservatively dressed and their faces were solemn.

This was not the first I had known of this small band of protestors. I'd seen them in television news programs. They were members of an off-branch religious group who were labeled as somewhat radical. They did call themselves Christians. The city was embarrassed by their demonstrations, but was legally unable to do anything about them. There, on the sidewalk, was Fred Phelps, the man we'd only heard about up until now—the "Minister of Hate."

He was related to almost everyone in his small congregation. He was surrounded by his wife, his children, and his grandchildren as he demonstrated at the park every Sunday afternoon. Phelps was well known in the area. He had even run for governor at one time. The purpose of his gatherings, and even of his political ambitions, was to spread the message of hell and damnation for homosexuals. I couldn't help wondering what might have happened in this man's lifetime to foster such contempt in him.

Even though I'd seen Phelps and his congregation on television before, the impact was much greater when I saw them in person. There are no words to describe how it feels to see six- and seven-year-old children carrying signs almost too big for them to manage, stating that "God hates fags!" and "Gays are going to hell!" The signs themselves were damaging enough, but that wasn't the worst part for me. I couldn't imagine teaching small children that kind of hate in the name of God. Their Sunday afternoons should be spent playing baseball or digging in the sand, not picketing against homosexuals. I wondered if they even understood what they were doing.

Other signs brought attention to those scriptures in the Bible that are so often used against gay and lesbian people. It's these scriptures, thrown in the faces of homosexuals, that are often responsible for their self-loathing and even suicides. I couldn't think of any place in the Bible that even remotely told us to teach that kind of hate to children. I prayed that none of this preacher's young flock was gay. The attitude they were raised with would surely destroy them, if they were. I prayed that people who were considering becoming Christians were not turning away, thinking that this was a representative of God's people. I thanked God that my son was gay and not a bigot.

The excitement and joy we'd felt after the afternoon's athletic events had been extinguished, like ice water on the Olympic flame. It made me think of the scripture in Matthew where we are told not to put our light under a bushel, but to let it shine in the world. When I saw those hate signs carried by children, I nearly cried. The beautiful potential for light from those children was being turned into the darkness of hate. It had a terrible, debilitating effect on me as the mother of a gay son when I saw those hateful words being paraded up and down the sidewalk at the park. I could only imagine how gay and lesbian people living in this city must have felt seeing this display of contempt, Sunday after Sunday. I thought of the families who had been forced to walk around the protestors to get to the funeral services of family members they'd loved, whose deaths were caused by AIDS.

As I thought about the scene I'd just witnessed, something Mary Borhek had written in her book, *Coming Out to Parents: A Two-Way Survival Guide for Lesbians and Gay Men and Their Parents* (Pilgrim Press, 1983), came to my mind. Ms. Borhek related a conversation she'd had with a fundamentalist friend about her book, *My Son Eric.* They were talking about being saved. Her friend asked her if she was concerned that the accepting attitudes she'd brought forth in her book might keep gays and lesbians from trying to change, thus causing them to be lost from salvation forever. She told him she had indeed given it much serious thought. Then she posed an interesting question to her friend: Ms. Borhek asked him if he had considered what consequences there might be on Judgment Day for those church people whose attitudes about same-sex relationships had kept millions of gay and lesbian people from having a close relationship with God. I understood her thinking and shared her concern that the church might be responsible for driving people away from God instead of sending them into a relationship with God.

It's my firm belief that we are here not only to let our own light shine in the world—the light of love—but to empower others to let theirs shine, as well. You can't do that in an atmosphere of hate. People can't develop those bright and shining qualities when they are being called names and told that they are going to hell for who they are. The flame will suffocate and go out, leaving everyone in the dark. Only by loving and accepting people as they are, unconditionally, can we keep from extinguishing the light so that ours can be a world of love—not one of darkness.

I'd found my sunglasses by now, but I didn't need them anymore. The sun had disappeared behind a cloud and the sky was overcast.

III
Opening
the Door

17

The Pediatrician

When your children are growing up, many different adults are important in their lives. Obviously, their parents are at the top of the list of meaningful and necessary individuals attending to their physical, emotional, and spiritual needs. Next would probably be grandparents and aunts and uncles. We were fortunate to have all of the above involved in our children's lives. These family members contributed many good things to our children's growing up.

If I were to choose one of the top "civilians," so to speak, who was a positive influence in the development and well-being of my children, it would be their pediatrician. We felt that ours was tops. More than once I saw him gently examine a crying, feverish child and then kiss him or her on the cheek in spite of the child's runny nose. He would then turn to the mother, put his hand on her shoulder, and deliver the diagnosis, followed by instructions necessary for the child's care and recovery.

As an added bonus, he would often peer over the top of the half-eyeglasses balanced precariously on the end of his nose and say, "…and how are *you* holding up, Mom?"

I can remember his policy on after-hours emergency calls. He would remind the parents that he had a family he liked to spend time with, but if they ever felt that their child was in jeopardy, they were not to hesitate to call him.

You could count on Dr. Jones to be committed to the children who had been entrusted to his care, but that didn't make him predictable. When Eric was eleven or so, he started complaining about a sore leg. This went on for quite some time. Eric was not one to complain about that sort of thing, so I decided it was a legitimate problem that needed looking into. I made an appointment.

Dr. Jones sat Eric up on the table and asked him a few questions. He tapped him on the knee with that funny little hammer that looks like a miniature tomahawk and turned to me with the verdict. I'll never forget what he said.

"Jesus didn't say we weren't going to have a little pain in our lives. It's growing pains. Eric's growing in fast spurts, and that causes what we call 'growing pains.' He'll be fine." Then he turned and walked out of the room.

I'm sure I must have blushed. I didn't know whether to laugh or just gather up my son and leave, so I did both. The doctor was right, of course. Eric was fine, and that was the end of that. I never forgot the quote, though.

Jesus didn't say we wouldn't have a little pain in our lives. I have thought of it often over the years.

When your children are grown, you don't have much occasion to see their pediatrician, so when we crossed paths at a mutual friend's party, we found it a good time to do some catching up. We talked about his son, who he said was doing well. Then he asked me how my young adult offspring were doing. He knew Eric was pursuing a career in acting, so I thought he would get a kick out of hearing that he was auditioning for a part on a TV soap opera.

It was then that the bomb dropped. I had hardly finished my sentence telling him what Eric was doing when he interrupted me with this statement:

"Those soap operas are all written by homosexuals, you know. That's why they're so full of sex. That's all homosexuals think about. They are grossly oversexed!"

This conversation was taking place in the kitchen of our friend's house. There were several small groups of people standing around chatting. When our conversation started, everyone else's stopped. They were looking our way, wide-eyed, and holding their collective breath.

I was caught off-guard. The potato chip I'd just swallowed was stuck like a wedge halfway down my throat. It was cutting off my breath. I felt as if someone had just hit me in the stomach. My knees buckled. I leaned hard against the counter so I wouldn't fall. I was afraid I was going to cry.

OK, Beverly, are you going to stand here and play dumb? Are you going to let this pass as if you agree with him? Can you risk defending the identity of your son? Can you risk not defending him?

I'd never spoken out against a put-down of homosexuals before, but suddenly I knew that that was what I had to do now. I didn't think anyone in the room knew what our situation was, so I thought I could pull this off without revealing anything. I knew I had to appear calm. I took a deep breath and crossed my arms tightly across my chest. With all the courage I could possibly gather, I began.

"Wait a minute, Dr. Jones. Do you know any homosexuals personally?"

"I don't need to know any personally. According to statistics...." His voice and attitude were cold.

"No, Dr. Jones"—I tried to be firm, but not overly emotional; I was afraid I'd give myself away—"not statistics. Faces. I'm talking about real live people with names and faces, people with jobs and families. There's a high percentage of gays in the arts, so we've met these people through Eric. These nice young men aren't statistics. They're human beings."

He continued his line of thinking as if I hadn't said a word.

"The statistics say they aren't interested in stable, committed relationships.

They're in bars and bathhouses picking up hundreds of partners, spreading disease. I tell you, all they think of is sex!"

"Dr. Jones, you are wrong! I know personal examples of young men and women who want caring, long-term, committed relationships, just like heterosexual couples. They aren't all in bars and bathhouses. I've seen them trying to make relationships work. Can you say that you know anyone personally in our town who is gay and behaving the way you describe?"

I realized that my shoulders had gotten tight and my whole body was tied in one big knot. I felt like the actor for a headache commercial. I took a deep breath and dropped my shoulders. I was wearing down and feeling as if my words were rising above Dr. Jones's head like cigarette smoke. I had to make one last effort though, before I gave up.

"I wish you could have the opportunity of meeting someone who is gay. If you ever do, I hope you will try to see him as a person and not as a stereotypical statistic. I think this conversation is over."

His voice, like mine, showed signs of resignation.

"I hope I haven't offended you."

Offended wasn't exactly the word I would have used, but a good substitute that could be used in front of the other guests wouldn't form in my brain. I mumbled something about having broad shoulders and walked away.

When I returned home after the party, I couldn't stop thinking about our conversation. When I thought of my son and of all the thousands of other gay and lesbian people out there in the world, I was saddened. I wanted to forget the ignorance and the prejudice and all the hateful things that had been said in my friend's kitchen. No matter how hard I tried, though, I couldn't ignore what had been said that night, nor could I help remembering two things that had been said to me so many years ago in the office of the man I had debated at the party.

"If you ever feel your child is in jeopardy, call me." *Dr. Jones, because of hate and prejudice he is always in jeopardy and so are the others.*

"Jesus didn't say we weren't going to have a little pain in our lives." *Dr. Jones, because of ignorance and a lack of understanding, he has a great deal of unnecessary pain in his life, and so do the others. I pray you never have to experience that kind of pain.*

Having been able to speak out against misinformation and narrow thinking that night for the first time, I realized that for me this was just the beginning of the process of coming out as a mother. Unwinding alone at the kitchen table with a cup of herbal tea, the room half-lit by the neighbor's yard light, I found myself responding to another of the doctor's familiar quotations.

"Yes, Dr. Jones, I'm holding up fine."

18

It's Moses' Fault

We read stories in the Bible over and over, enjoying their   colorful characters and the dramatic settings and circumstances in which they unfold. We wrestle with the language and the history important to their meaning. We teach them to our children and tell them that this is what life is all about.

These stories are all well and good, if we can keep them at a distance, not having to deal with their relevance in our personal lives. We don't mind pointing an accusing finger at Adam and Eve for their weakness in plucking the tempting fruit from the forbidden tree, as long as we don't have to be held accountable for our own disobedience. What about Noah? Now, there was a talented boat builder! Although we joke about building arks during the rainy season on the plains, few of us dig out our cubit sticks or call the lumberyard about cypress wood when the storm clouds begin to form in the sky. We can't imagine doing something as bizarre as Noah did, just because God asked us to.

Although these two Bible stories are important in my life, neither has had the impact, much to my surprise and even distress, as another one has had. From August of 1992 until January of 1993, Moses of Exodus and Beverly of the Midwest had a lot in common. We had both had the experience of struggling with what God might be asking us to do, and what our answers would be.

In review, this is what happened to Moses. He was going along, minding his own business, feeling kind of down about the way the Egyptians were treating the Israelites. The Pharaoh was being cruel and ruthless in his treatment of that particular group of people—the slaves he had working in horrible, inhumane conditions, building pyramids for him. Their lives weren't considered worth much. Now, this bothered Moses a lot, but what could he do?

God knew what needed to be done, and sometimes got real creative in communicating with people, letting them know what was in store to remedy a particular situation. This is what happened between God and Moses when the Almighty appeared to our hero by way of a burning bush. God told Moses he was needed to help deliver the Israelites from their bondage. Of course, Moses was totally unprepared for this. He did what any one of us would have done:

he started making excuses.

"I'm just a common person. I don't have what it takes to deal with people like the Pharaoh. I can't talk to someone like that. I don't have the authority. If I tell him about the burning bush, he'll laugh me right out of the palace—maybe even call me crazy."

Well, God didn't take "no" for an answer. Moses got a rod that had special power and Aaron to help with the talking, and then he got put to work.

It took a long time to get the Israelites delivered. Unfortunately, Moses didn't get to go with them over the line to the land of milk and honey, but he did have the satisfaction of telling God "yes." He did the best he could with what he had and he did it faithfully, and that is all God really asked him to do.

What does this have to do with Beverly Cole—wife, mother, clerk in a college bookstore, and amateur writer? In the six months from August 1992 to January 1993, I got a feel for what Moses might have gone through because I was getting some strong nudges about what I was supposed to be doing at this particular time in my life and I was fighting it tooth and nail. This is how it went for me:

Second week in August 1992: During this week I was enrolled in a journal-writing class at the University of Minnesota, Duluth. In one of my journal entries, I revealed to the class that I have a son who is gay. Later in the week, at my individual student conference, Phoebe, the instructor, asked me if I'd ever considered doing some writing about our family and how we had come to acceptance of our son's gayness. I told her I hadn't considered publishing anything I'd written. I just wrote for my own entertainment, certainly not to share something as personal as our family struggle with homosexuality.

"There's a real need for it, Beverly. I believe you could do it, and so many families are hurting. Think about it. OK?"

"Sure, but I can't make any promises."

When I got home, the idea kept eating at me but I couldn't bring myself to take it seriously. I did pray about it a couple of times, but didn't really want an answer.

September: In September, I started my second year in a Jungian dream interpretation class led by a local Presbyterian minister. We talked about how God guided people in their dreams in the Bible, and that it still happened today if we were open to seeking God's will in our lives. Whatever people might be struggling with in their waking life is often addressed in their dreams. That's what happened to me. In my dreams I began to get nudges, willing or not. I had two dreams that I interpreted like this:

September 12: The first dream was about returning to college. Two things stood out for me in this dream. When it came time to pay the tuition fees required to start back to school, I was told that there was a discount if I'd been reading books. That thought struck a sensitive spot in an area I continuously struggled with in my effort to live a Christian life: I loved *reading about* having compassion and helping people in need, but I didn't always get around to acting on that compassion. That was discounted, short-changed Christian living.

The second image that I felt needed my attention in this dream was a ragged and dirty man with a scruffy beard and compelling blue eyes. When our eyes met in the dream, I felt somehow drawn to the poor and oppressed of the world. The man's presence directed my attention away from general thinking about helping the oppressed to having a specific needy person in front of me. The dream didn't show me specifically *which* poor and oppressed I might seek out, but a second dream did.

September 24: Nearly two weeks later, I had another dream. There were several things that caught my attention in this dream.

I was in front of a pizza restaurant. I was talking to a pizza delivery man. It was this man I most identified with in the dream. The word "delivery" kept coming back into my mind as I searched for what meaning might be present in this scene.

My son was also in this dream. He was wearing a bright pink cape and was making exaggerated, stereotypically gay effeminate moves with it. I knew in the dream that he was indeed gay. Then he climbed into the back of the pizza delivery truck that was parked on the street and began stuffing leftover pizza garbage into his mouth. This was distressing to me. Eric eating other people's garbage.

The third element that stayed in my mind was a strong feeling—a feeling of fear. When Eric climbed down from the truck and left the scene to go change his clothes, I was terrified that someone had seen him and would find him and stab him because he was gay.

As I thought about this dream combined with the one I'd had just a few nights before, I felt that there was a message for me. Perhaps the oppressed I'd wondered about before were indeed members of the gay community. After all, their lives are often filled with the "garbage" handed out by a society lacking in knowledge and understanding of the real lives of gay and lesbian people. Perhaps my dreams were encouraging me to answer the spiritual call to help restore wholeness to a broken people who have had to settle for scraps for so long. *When I was hungry, you gave me food.*

It was becoming clear to me, like it or not, that what Phoebe had moved in Minnesota, God had seconded in my sleep. My speech would be my words on paper, and my rod would be my pencil. I would give it a try.

Mid-October: By mid-October I had two or three chapters in mind for a book, but I needed some statistics and other official information, so I called a counselor I knew was working with gay and lesbian clients. Along with the information I'd asked for, she gave me a book I hadn't seen before. It was written by a gay man in a metropolitan area who started right out describing the full range of the worst behavior found in the gay community. He described crude, obnoxious, obscene actions. He outlined relationships that were unfeeling and filled with heartless behavior I'd not seen and had not wanted to deal with, or to admit even existed. I totally fell apart. I put the book away and just sat and cried. I don't like to look at the dark side of any segment of society, gay or straight—kind of an ostrich syndrome. I began to have doubts. What was I doing? Did I really know who I was defending? How many gay people did I actually know? I felt sick and confused.

To make matters worse, I had set up a time to talk to the gay support group that met at one of the local counseling centers. Some had agreed to do interviews for me, telling their stories and sharing their lives. I began to panic. I couldn't back out on these men and women. Their lives were full of people who had backed out on them. I couldn't do it, too. On the other hand, what if I went and found out that all of these negative things I'd read were true? The more I thought about it, though, the more I knew there really wasn't a choice. I had to go and take my chances.

November 8: I talked to Dale and he said he would go with me to the support group meeting. I swallowed a couple of antacids I had in my medicine cabinet for an upset stomach and we headed out.

It was a crisp Sunday evening. Several men were gathered in the parking lot, smoking cigarettes before the meeting. *You are the only gay person I know who doesn't smoke.* That life-changing comment I'd heard just before Christmas several years before came to my mind. We slipped past the group, muttering some kind of greeting, and made our way up the stairs to the room where we would meet. A young man took our coats and asked if we would like a soda. We declined and sat down within a circle of folding chairs. People kept drifting in. Finally, the meeting started.

There was a business meeting first, and a man whose voice had stereotypically gay inflections talked about making a public service announcement on the radio. He complained that he had tried to sound "butch" or straight, but his voice had betrayed him. Everyone laughed. I had never thought about what a problem that must be for some gay men. As the meeting continued, Michael, the group president, introduced us. I decided to clear things up right away, so I confessed that I wasn't going to do the book as originally planned. I said I didn't want our life on a public bookshelf. I made my apology and told them I'd decided I was just somebody's mother—I didn't write books and I didn't get in the middle of controversy. If they were disappointed at my decision, it wasn't apparent. They were very gracious.

From that point on, it was just a matter of sharing our lives, our different experiences, and the things we had in common. We told them what it was like being parents of a gay child, and they told us what it was like being gay in their families and in society. Many of the stories were touching, some were sad, some eye-opening.

Two different men had been discharged from the military because someone had found out they were gay and they hadn't lied when confronted. One was in the army for fourteen years with a spotless record and high reviews. Neither was awarded any benefits when he left.

Many had lost the love of their families. Others had families who knew they were gay, but just didn't talk about it. One young man had makeup on and showed a cutting, rather sarcastic sense of humor. He said that in the little town where he came from they didn't even say the "G" word. At first he was a little unsettling to us, but as the evening went on we came to appreciate his colorful personality. We also began to realize that his wit served him well in covering his feelings.

There was a man who had turned fifty-five before he finally was able to admit to himself that he was gay. There were men who'd been married and had children in an attempt to fool others and themselves. There were those who had been involved with drugs and alcohol to deaden the pain. Three couples—two male and one female—were looking forward to holy unions coming up in the spring and summer. The lesbian women who were there humored us as we referred to the group as "you guys." We told them that was our generic terminology and they just laughed with us every time we stuck our foot in our mouths. One couple had been together for eleven years and had kept the relationship going while each lived in a different state because of professional obligations.

The evening flew by, and when we left it was with a burden lifted from our shoulders. We had seen a more diverse gay community than we had known before, and we had liked the people we met. We'd shared in one another's life stories, whether tragic or triumphant. We had a special bond somehow. I had a feeling we would see more of these people from time to time in the future. I hoped so. I realized then, in real honesty, that when you say you're willing to accept a certain group of people, you have to think in terms of everyone, not just certain ones that fit your mold. I had some work to do on my own attitude before I could even think about doing any more writing, but I wasn't giving up yet, either. Geraldo would have to wait awhile for my book tour appearance, though. I was still very short on courage.

I did go home and finish reading the controversial book that had so upset me in the first place. When I read further into the book, I learned that the author was calling the irresponsible segments of the gay community to clean up their act and for those who were living normal, reputable lives to come out of the closet so that the world would know the whole story. I felt better. It's dark and it hurts your eyes when your head is buried in the sand. I still wasn't ready to go ahead with the book. I didn't think I had the courage. Dale kept telling me I would do it when I was ready.

January 24, 1993: Sometimes we are given what we need without our even being aware of it. My courage was provided in an event that started one Sunday afternoon on the pages of the social section of the newspaper. One of the couples from the support group announced their wedding in the local newspaper and was featured in a full-page article. The editorials started flooding the newspaper and there were opinions all the way from "Run them out of town" to "What's the big deal, anyway?" When some of the most negative ones started showing up in print, I could stand it no longer. I wrote the following editorial in support of the couple and of their minister, sent it into the paper, and waited.

It's About Love

Our town has certainly been buzzing of late about the first gay couple "coming out" into our small city society by announcing their marriage in the local newspaper. The public and private reactions have covered a wide range of emotions. We really shouldn't be surprised at the stir it has caused. This is a first for our city, and certainly takes some getting used to. Let's try, however, to take a moment to look at this situation, not emotionally but from "people" perspective.

Steven and Skip are two gay males who have been through hell trying to conform to a heterosexual society. They tried marrying women and having children, to fit into the mold everyone else in society said was right for them. They ended up with broken homes, drug and alcohol problems, and suicide attempts. They were trying to live a lie.

If you are a heterosexual male or female reading this article, try to think of yourself in a same-sex relationship. "Impossible," you say. I rest my case. These guys have finally come to accept themselves as they truly are—gay males. They have had the courage to stick their necks out to try to help our homophobic society understand. They have been willing to take the heat to show their children that committed relationships are important. Not only have these men finally been able to love and be loved by another valuable human being, but they are setting an example of committed, monogamous relationships, not the irresponsibility in relationships that has caused so much suffering in both the gay and straight communities.

What about this minister, Bob Lay? He actually performed the marriage ceremony for these gay men. He's not the first person in history who was willing to buck a rule-oriented, condemning society. He isn't the first who looked at an individual as a whole, worthy human being and loved him unconditionally. Jesus did that, and he tried to teach you and me to do that, too. Bob Lay preaches love—love for people and between people. Bob Lay is practicing what he preaches. We may not always know what all the rules are, but we do know what the most important one is. It's love. Jesus was crucified for his stand on loving. Let's not crucify Bob Lay. Haven't we learned from our mistakes?

Our lives are so complicated in these confusing times. It's hard to understand everything we deal with in our various situations. The one thing that does make things easier for all of us is to look at life and remember—it's about love.

I was braced for the worst to happen, but it didn't. The day the editorial came out, my phone rang all day long with calls of support. When I went to church on Sunday, I got hugs and congratulations. It felt great.

January 31: On that same Sunday afternoon, there was a combination parent support group and gay support meeting. We talked and shared stories as usual. When I had my turn on the floor, I announced that I was writing the book and that it would be finished this time. There was a muted *Yes!* behind me, coming from one of the gay men I'd met at our first meeting. I turned to see an ear-to-ear grin from the person in the seat behind me.

I didn't know if we would reach the promised land of acceptance and understanding in my lifetime. I'd be eighty-nine in forty years. At any rate, I was ready to take my chances and give it a shot. Moses didn't seem to be any the worse for wear. Maybe I could make it, too. Besides, I was sure God was tired of bugging me and ready to move on to nudging someone else.

19
The Good Book

The Bible, alias "the Good Book," has been around for centuries. It has stood the test of time and has remained on the best-seller list ahead of many other types of literature, old and new. It has been the subject of more controversial discussions—even debates—than any other book ever written. Even amid all the dissension it remains, for many people, a book of unshakable truths that guide and influence their lives. This positive force has the potential for making them richer, more life-giving individuals. For others, it's a book that condemns and judges, robbing them of the quality of love and life they feel they deserve.

Gay and lesbian people, especially, have been the targets of disgust and even hate from those who would use the Bible's guidance to justify such feelings. Moral judgment and condemnation are said to be acceptable in the eyes of those individuals who would use certain selected scriptures from the pages of this sacred book to support that hate.

Because I was thrown into the middle of the homosexual issue on a personal level, I wanted very much to understand what the scriptures being used to support condemnation of gays had to say. In some instances, those scriptures have become a matter of life and death for members of the gay community. They have, on occasion, been used as "permission" for gay bashing.

I understood these passages well enough for my own personal satisfaction, but I needed to clarify the information in my mind in order to articulate what I'd learned for the book I was writing.

Just reading the scriptures on my own wasn't always enough. I found it more beneficial to discuss them with others who were more knowledgeable about the history and language involved in Bible study than I was. As I talked with people who were familiar with the language and customs of biblical times, it became apparent that there was more to understanding its message than just the words written on the pages.

In each of the Old Testament stories commonly used against gays, understanding the Jewish culture—their social and religious customs—was of utmost importance to the interpretation of the stories. This applies also to issues involving women. Standards like the negative attitude of that patriarchal society toward women, considering them "possessions," made a big difference in how people's lives were lived. One of the stories from the Bible makes that point in a subtle way. That story, Sodom and Gomorrah, is the one also used most often in the case against the "sin" of homosexuality. A review of that story might be helpful before proceeding.

The story begins with a man named Lot, who was a citizen of the city of Sodom. Lot was sitting near the gates of that city one evening when two strangers, angels from God, made their way through those gates. The messengers had been sent by God to verify rumors of out-of-control sin in Sodom. Lot jumped to his feet in order to give proper greeting to the men who were passing through that area. His greeting probably went something like this:

"Welcome to Sodom. I greet you in the name of the Lord. Come and take a meal at my house and spend the night before you continue your journey."

The strangers were reluctant at first, as they had planned to spend the night in the streets of Sodom, but Lot's hospitality proved irresistible. He took them to his house, where they ate and prepared to go to bed. Lot was about to put out the lamp when he heard a commotion outside his house. The men of the town, young and old, were gathered in his yard and were shouting something. When he went out to investigate, he couldn't believe what he heard.

"We have come about your guests. Bring them out to us so we might have sex with them."

Lot responded quickly, in a manner that would not have been unusual in that time and in that culture.

"No," he said. "They are safe under the shelter of my roof. Take my two virgin daughters instead. Do whatever you like with them, but leave my guests alone."

The townsmen pushed against Lot, calling for the release of the aliens who had come to their city to judge them. He was caught in the doorway, and it seemed as if he would be unable to stop their advance. The angels came to his rescue, pulling him inside to safety. They struck the unruly men blind so that they couldn't find the doorway. Several verses later, God concludes that the rumors of excessive sin in Sodom are true, and makes the decision to destroy it, making a wide sweep that takes Gomorrah as well. Lot was rewarded for his care of the angels with a pre-warning that allowed him and his family to flee the city ahead of the destruction.

People who use this story to condemn gay people say that God's decision to destroy the cities was made because of sin that was taking place there, especially the sin of homosexuality. It is true that the desire for the act of homosexuality in this story was sinful. Had Lot turned his houseguests over to the crowd for sex, the action would have been rape, an act degrading under any circumstances, but especially in this culture and time in history. Here is where we begin to look at the scripture in that context.

Earlier, we mentioned the attitude of this culture toward women. Females were considered possessions, owned by men like slaves, to be used in whatever manner the men might choose. Women had no status. If a man became the victim of homosexual rape, that would force him to play the role of a woman. He would be without power, under the control of another man. There was no worse humiliation to be endured in that male-dominated, patriarchal society. No one could possibly endorse treating guests in such a degrading manner. It would be rude, downright inhospitable. This is an important point in the story that shouldn't be overlooked. It is the sin of inhospitality.

Some people would debate the importance "hospitality" holds in this story, but as I struggled to be clear on the interpretation, I couldn't help thinking about the scripture in the New Testament where Jesus implores us to love and nurture strangers who might show up on our doorstep by giving them food, drink, and clothing. He says that in serving these, we have served him. Of course, Jesus wasn't in the picture yet, but we who have the entire Bible to call upon know the high favor in which hospitality was held by our Lord.

In continuing to wrestle with priorities in the interpretation of the Sodom and Gomorrah story, I couldn't overlook an aspect of the story that people who use this scripture against gays so often seem to ignore. When the townsmen came to Lot and asked him to give the strangers to them, he offered his virgin daughters instead. He seemed to have no qualms about offering the young women to be raped by an entire community of men. Amazing! In today's society, the daughters would be in court in a minute, pressing charges against their father for abuse. Obviously, our times and mores are drastically different from those in which this event occurred. What's especially surprising to me is that critics of homosexuality today are willing to overlook this abomination as evidence of a culture whose values would be entirely foreign to us today, but don't think twice about using the story as a basis for condemning the lives of gay people. They demand an updated respect for women, especially when it comes to sexual exploitation, and yet their attitudes about homosexuality remain in the dark ages.

Other scriptures make reference to men lying with men and assert that it is wrong. These scriptures are particularly disturbing to readers. Let's take a look at that concept from the standpoint of the procreative attitudes of the time. It was important for the survival of the tribes of the Hebrew nation that the population be increased, that many Hebrew children be born. The sacred male semen, the seed of future generations, was not to be squandered in situations that did not produce offspring. Engaging in homosexual activity, by their culture's standards, was an extravagant spilling of that life-giving fluid. It was sinful.

If we look closely at all of the scriptures used against homosexuality, it is apparent that the concepts of a homosexual "orientation" and homosexual love were not part of the knowledge of the times. When references are made to natural and unnatural sex acts, all that is understood is the "act" itself, and, as we have seen, it carried with it some heavy cultural baggage. This being the case, the people's lack of knowledge about differences in sexual orientations leaves some unanswered questions. If the characters in the Bible passages who were committing the homosexual acts were heterosexual, their actions *were* unnatural. Since homosexual orientation was probably not understood at that time, it certainly leaves the door open for questions about what "natural" really meant, or didn't mean, to those recording the original circumstances.

I needed to answer one last question in my writing about the Bible and homosexuality, but it wouldn't take up much space. The question was, "What did Jesus say about the subject?" The answer was *Nothing.*

All of this was very helpful. It made sense to me personally and was good information for the book, but I felt an underlying restlessness I couldn't shake. A person can debate scripture until blue in the face, but if the Holy Spirit isn't working through those passages, to make positive changes in our lives, what good does it do to figure it out? Somehow, for me, just being able to defend homosexuality through a reinterpretation of the scriptures wasn't what this was all about. I felt that there was more to be learned from digging around in the Old and New Testaments while thinking about homosexuality. Something was bugging me, but what?

Help came one afternoon when my doorbell rang. I opened the door to a longtime friend who stood on my front porch grinning her familiar, ornery grin. Her Italian heritage was evident in her dark eyes and black hair, which was only beginning to gray. She wasn't very tall, but what she lacked in height, she made up for in spunk.

"Aren't you going to let a poor soul in out of the heat?"

Carmen had been a friend of our family for nearly twenty years. Although she was now in her sixties, she was full of life. She always had been. You always knew she was up to something, as she had some kind of a service project going most of the time. Today was no exception.

As I let her in, I asked, "What are you up to? I didn't know you were going to be in town today." I directed her to the recliner in the family room.

"You know you can't get rid of me. You just never know when I might show up on your doorstep. Hope I didn't catch you at a bad time. I was passing through town and stopped to pick up the stuff for the VOSH scholarship garage sale." She made her way to the family room and sat down in the recliner, pushing it back to raise the footrest.

"It's not a bad time. I was needing a break anyway. Our stuff is boxed up in the garage. I'll get it for you later. Can I get you something to drink, Carm?"

"Some ice water would be great, thanks. What's all this?" She pointed to the piles of Bibles and reference books scattered all over the floor.

I handed her the water and explained. "I've been looking up scriptural references all morning and trying to figure out how to present the ones on homosexuality for my book, but I'm having trouble. I'm feeling unsettled. I started out looking up all of the references about homosexuality to get them organized. I wanted to help my readers understand what they say. I just needed to review them. I'm comfortable with the basic scriptures, but I just keep feeling like all this fits into a bigger picture somehow. I'm missing something, but I don't know what."

"What do you mean? What are you looking at?"

Carmen had an extensive background in Bible study and had been my mentor as well as my friend. She lived her life immersed in scripture and committed to trying to follow the Holy Spirit's leading. I had the greatest respect and admiration for her, both as a person and for her knowledge of the Bible. I was glad to have the opportunity to run my questions past her.

"Well, Carmen, it just seems like there's so much in the Bible that's used negatively against people. I see it used with such hurtfulness and judgment. It's so narrow and limiting. Jesus' message was much different, freer and more inclusive. I'm sure of that myself, but how can I make it clear to those who would keep gays from feeling accepted by God by using the Bible against them? So many people say they'll accept them but add, 'only if they are celibate.' Others require them to change their sexual orientation. That's crazy."

I knew she would agree. I'd grown into many of my attitudes under her influence.

"I agree with you, Beverly, and what I think it all boils down to is the difference between the laws given to the people through Moses and the ones given to the people through Jesus. I'll show you what I mean. Look up Exodus 20 and start reading."

That was easy enough—second book of the Bible.

Thou shalt have no other gods before me.

Thou shalt make no graven images.

Thou shalt not kill.

Thou shalt not commit adultery.

Thou shalt not steal.
Thou shalt not, thou shalt not.
I looked up and waited for an explanation, but got further instruction instead.
"Now turn to Matthew 5. Read the Beatitudes to me."

Blessed are the poor in spirit, for theirs is the kingdom of heaven.

Blessed are those who mourn, for they shall be comforted.

Blessed are the meek, for they shall inherit the earth.

I read aloud until I'd finished the first twelve verses. "How far should I go?" I asked.

"Go ahead and read the rest of it to yourself, but especially pay attention to the seventeenth verse." She waited patiently while I read.

The heading above the section starting with the seventeenth verse is entitled "The Higher Righteousness." Verse seventeen is the one about Jesus not coming to abolish the laws but to fulfill them. By the heading given, I thought that probably meant he hadn't come to get rid of the law, but to bring a new dimension to it, a new revelation—that higher righteousness indicated in the heading.

The next section heading was "Anger and Reconciliation." In it, Jesus reminded his followers of the old commandment not to kill, but added some new thoughts about attitudes. He called for a mindset of reconciliation instead of anger when dealing with one's brother. He said a gift at the altar was of no value if it was offered while there was unresolved anger in the heart of the giver.

The next section was headed with these words: "Adultery and Divorce." Again, Jesus called for a close look at the attitudes of his flock. The act of committing adultery was already taboo, but Jesus went on to say that looking at a woman with lust in one's heart was just as bad.

It was becoming clear to me that Jesus expected his committed followers to take stock of their feelings toward their fellow man, to look into their own hearts. Worthy attitudes were as important as worthy actions.

I began to see what Carmen might have in mind in comparing the Ten Commandments with the Beatitudes. Moses was known for always laying down laws. He had to be tough to deal with the Israelites. They needed rules and regulations. Maybe that's why the Ten Commandments were stated so strongly with "Thou shalt nots." The message needed to be crystal clear as to what was expected of them. They had to understand God's authority and learn to obey his laws in order to survive in the wilderness as well as to keep their faith.

Jesus, on the other hand, came to reveal a different side of God with a somewhat different agenda. Presenting the rules with "Blessed are those who…" sets us up for what Jesus had been sent to do. It was more positive, more reconciling. He was sent to teach us how to use those rules to love God and each other, not just for survival. *Love the Lord your God with all your heart, and your neighbor as yourself.* That's very likely to require an attitude change, but the result is bound to be more quality in our lives and in our relationship with God. It was all beginning to fall into place.

Carmen interrupted my thoughts.

"Now, here's another thing to think about. This might help you in dealing with people who can't see past their opinion of homosexuals as less than acceptable people. Nowhere in the Bible—and I mean not one place—does Jesus ever ask anyone to be anything other than who or what he or she is. I'll say it again. Nowhere in the Bible does Jesus ask anyone to be anything other than who or what he or she is. He even called each of his disciples to follow him just as they were, including a despised tax collector. He associated with women and valued their friendships as highly as the men's. He even valued women's opinions—unheard of in that day. He didn't say you had to be Jew to receive the good news. He just made it clear: Blessed are those who receive the good news and use it for good. Do you see what I'm getting at?" My friend took a drink of water after finishing her mini-sermon.

"You know, Carm, that affirmation just cleared up something else for me. A friend, who thought she was helping, wrote to me about Eric being gay. She told me Satan had perverted what God had created, causing him to 'live a homosexual lifestyle.' She went on to say that Jesus had died on the cross so that Eric's sins could be forgiven. I agree that Jesus did die on the cross for Eric's sins, along with everyone else's. Jesus died on the cross so that whatever things in Eric's life needed "fixing" could be fixed. But who Eric really is—a homosexual male person—can stay the same. You've been a great help, as usual. Thanks, Carmen. You always come through when I need you the most."

My problem was solved. Somehow Carmen had helped me find what was missing.

I knew now that my chapter covering the scriptures on homosexuality couldn't be limited to explaining what we know concerning history and social custom in biblical times. That was indeed necessary, but my resource material said so much more. I couldn't leave my readers with just the differences in interpretation and understanding of the Bible verses. I had to share a bit of the good news from that holy book, the news of love that is accepting and uplifting—the love that brings out the best in individuals and societies—love that builds them up and makes them better people—love that brings them together instead of driving them apart. I had to let my readers—gay and straight—know that for God to love them, they don't have to be anything or anyone except who they are. *Blessed are they.*...It's true. It says so in the Good Book.

IV
Stepping Out

20

Battleships, Tugboats, and Canoes

When members of a family are faced with a loved one's terminal illness, there are emotional stages that are necessary for them to go through in order to deal with that illness and with the loved one's inevitable death. These milestones along the path of acceptance must be met in order to be able to let the dying relative go—so he or she can take the journey from this life into the next. The patient, too, must spend time within each of these stages of emotional turmoil in order to be ready to go. It is generally recognized that there are five of these stages.

The five stages needed to deal with death and dying—denial and isolation, anger, bargaining, depression, and finally acceptance—are in many cases the same five stages that parents of gay and lesbian children must go through in order to find healing.

For the family of someone who has a disease, the process starts at the moment the doctor gives them the final diagnosis, usually following a long period of medical testing. "I'm sorry, there's nothing we can do."

For the family of a homosexual child, it begins from the moment that child comes out of the closet, when he shares a new part of who he is with the ones he loves. "Mom, Dad, there's something I have to tell you—I'm gay."

The stages of dealing with these two situations may be similar, but there are two important differences. With a truly terminal illness, there is little hope, if any, for survival. It's fatal. In having a gay child, there is hope—and everyone can survive. Many parents who have just learned of their child's different sexual orientation may not think that this is so, but it is. In both situations, the most important ingredient for healing emotions is time.

Carolyn Welch Griffin, Marian J. Wirth, and Arthur G. Wirth, co-authors of *Beyond Acceptance: Parents of Lesbians and Gays Talk About Their Experiences* (Prentice Hall, 1983), write about the levels of understanding families have to go through if they are going to be able to accept their gay offspring. This book deals with many families and their journeys through those levels of understanding to acceptance and beyond.

111

The first level of understanding presented in the book is *self-centered concern*. In this first level, parents deal with the initial news of their child's gayness with a wide range of emotions. These emotions may come out in any order and in varying degrees of intensity, but they are very real. Some parents can't handle the news at first, and head straight for the comfort of denial. When that doesn't ease the pain, anger may explode onto the scene, shame and depression may follow, and on their coattails, a large dose of guilt.

It's always a time of loss and confusion. All the hopes and dreams parents have tied up in their children are pending. All of their plans and visions of the future come crashing down onto their heads. Many think they are going crazy; some wish they would, so they could get it over with.

Parents begin to blame each other, and then they blame the child. Their child's growing-up years all pass before them and every parenting mistake they ever made is mentally circled in red.

When you lose a child to death, your community is at your doorstep with food, support, and love. When you "lose" your child to a sexual orientation—one completely foreign to you and to most of society—you dare not ask for help.

Level One is the hardest stage of all in this strange adjustment process, because it hurts so much and there's no place to go for the pain. Family members need to be especially patient with one another during this time of mourning. There is no quick fix. It takes time—sometimes years—to work through the initial shock. It's hard for the gay child to be patient, because by being ready to "come out" to his family, he himself is ready to move on. He or she may have already spent years working through the issue. It's hard to wait while everyone else catches up.

There's danger in this level of understanding when parents get stuck in any of these negative emotions. If one or both parents fail to see their way clear to proceed, it can make them sick; it can make the entire family sick. The emotions need to be recognized and dealt with if Level Two is ever to be reached.

Level Two is of *child-centered concern*. On this plane, the parents have dealt with many of their own concerns and are ready and willing to move on to those issues that are being dealt with by their child. They may be neither thrilled that their child is gay nor comfortable with the sexual issues, but they are ready to do the best they can to give emotional sanctuary to their child. Society, in many areas, has turned its back on homosexuals, so their families must turn their faces toward them.

This is a time when families begin to realize that they don't have very much information on homosexuality, and what they do have is probably inaccurate or dated. They begin to read whatever they can find on the subject and they ask their gay children questions. This communication also helps to restore parent-child relationships.

At this level, parents may find themselves comfortable enough to risk sharing their situation with a few close friends—to test the waters, so to speak. Sometimes grandparents are told, but not always. That varies from family to family.

A desire to talk to other parents may surface at this time, for reasons of fellowship, support, and information-sharing. Exchanging stories is often helpful. Families don't feel that they are the only ones going through the ordeal when they hear that others have had similar experiences.

A few brave souls may even have the courage to speak up in media situations, but usually anonymously or using first names only. Prejudice against gays is beginning to bother them, and doubts creep in concerning society's negative views on the subject.

Level Three is set on a broader base yet—one of *concern for all gays and lesbians and their parents.*

There is a new-found feeling of freedom involved in Level Three. Parents have usually met a number of gay and lesbian people by this time, and have grown to appreciate them as worthy and unique individuals. Because there are now names and faces connected to the issue, a new urgency develops in fighting the social injustices put upon those in the gay community. Parents no longer care what others think, and they speak out. They don't hesitate to call someone on the carpet for degrading homosexuals by making them the brunt of jokes.

By this time, they are sure of their facts and face opposing points of view head-on. Opportunities are not passed by when homosexuality comes up in conversation, and the situation lends itself to educating those who might not know the facts.

Level Three might be called the stage of acceptance and beyond. It's at this level that positive action must be sown in order to reap positive results.

It's been my experience, in many years of working on various kinds of committees, that the differences in personalities, gifts, talents, and methods of operation are invaluable in getting things done. All that is needed is a common goal toward which everyone can aim. It's no different with educating society in the area of homosexuality. It's a matter of blooming where you are planted and doing what you have the power to do, but there are different ways of accomplishing the same goal. Let me illustrate this with the following analogy. I'll use three types of water vessels to make my point: battleships, tugboats, and canoes.

Battleship—*Any of a class of modern warships of the largest size, carrying the greatest number of guns and batteries and clad with the heaviest armor.*

What does this definition have to do with gay rights? Those who might identify themselves with the "battleships" in the fight for gay rights and acceptance are those whose personalities and drives put them in front positions, with maximum exposure. These are the people who are blessed with, and comfortable using, speaking skills in front of audiences—informing, educating, exposing, and maybe even preaching a little about the gay community and its concerns. This group includes gay activists and gay activist-parents whose talents call them in this direction. It's these people whose faces might be seen on national television, marching in a gay pride parade.

Tugboat—*A powerful small boat designed for towing larger vessels.*

The tugboats are those who form the strong support for the larger vessels. This action translates into writing congressmen, speaking out in defense of gays at social gatherings and at dinner parties. These medium-sized vessels might even be organizing education classes in their local churches, forcing them to re-think the difficult issue of homosexuality and encouraging them to re-evaluate attitudes and judgments. You can count on many of them for the money needed to keep the battleships afloat.

Canoe—*A light, slender boat with pointed ends, propelled by paddles.*

Don't let words like "light" and "slender" fool you as to the strength and value of this quiet little vessel's part in promoting understanding and acceptance. This silent partner has ends that are pointed to subtly poke and prod, getting things done as it glides along.

Those who fit this category might be writing editorials, articles, even books, to bring the issue before the public eye. They, like the tugboats, may be sending in monetary contributions to support those who are on the front lines.

These quiet but committed members of the fleet may also be found nurturing—a much-needed quality sometimes in short supply for gays and lesbians and their families.

People in all three groups will probably be members of PFLAG (Parents and Friends of Lesbians and Gays), a national organization formed to support families and friends of gays and lesbians. This organization is invaluable in getting helpful information to them for healing.

Finding out that they have a gay son or daughter, brother or sister, nephew or niece, grandson or granddaughter, is a huge shock for families—one not easily dealt with and not quickly resolved. Time is a gift families need to give themselves so they might be patient and gentle with one another. It takes time, lots of it, to come to grips with that knowledge and then to decide what to do with it.

It's been several years since we found out Eric was gay. The sea of understanding has been rough and turbulent at times, hard to navigate. The journey is not one you rush through or take lightly. The main objective at times is just to stay afloat. There's a reward in making the effort, though—in learning, accepting, and, finally, sharing. When the wind dies down and the waves settle around you, the water is calm and crystal clear. You can see all the way to the bottom. With faith, community, and family to see you through the turbulence, there's a reconciling peace that binds you all together as nothing else on earth can do. You can see your way clear for smooth sailing for yourself and, ultimately, for many others.

21
Paths and Bridges

I was sitting in a Sunday school class at my church one Sunday morning, listening to a lesson on world religions. The particular religion we were studying was Hinduism. The facilitator of the class had spent part of his childhood in Indonesia where there had been a strong Hindu influence. He shared with us his experience of going to the town square to see puppet shows where the stories in Hindu mythology were acted out on stage. He described puppets that were dressed in colorful and elaborate costumes and had grim and horrible faces. He told us of his childhood wonder and delight as he was pulled into the battles of the characters who represented the duality of good and evil.

In the discussion that followed, we tried to relate that same conflict of good vs. evil as we examined our own Christian faith. Although Christianity and Hinduism are worlds apart in our dogma (the body of theological doctrines), there are similarities in our stories and some of our values.

One of the ladies in the class who, as a longtime children's Sunday school teacher, was well versed on the stories in the Bible, voiced a profound observation she'd made over the years. "You know, it's been my experience that dogma divides and stories unite. Jesus was aware of that when he came down so hard on all of the religious rules and regulations that were so strongly adhered to in Jewish society in his day. Instead of lessons in 'dogma,' Jesus chose to tell stories."

I couldn't help but think about the conflict I'd lived with for the past several years—my own story of personal struggle with trying to reconcile homosexuality and my Christian faith. It seemed to me that I was starting to hear and see evidence that perhaps the broader Christian community was ready to struggle with that conflict, too. It's an area of great controversy, making it hard for churches to know how best to deal with it. There is difficulty in finding appropriate ways of introducing homosexual studies into educational materials and curriculums. We wrestle with our hesitance, questioning whether it's scriptural or if we need to look honestly at our own homophobia (fear and hatred of lesbians and gay men). The assumption, however, is that as the body of Christ, we all want to live our lives according to the example of love Jesus showed us. We can't fool ourselves into thinking we are actually living that way if anyone is being denied a hospitable welcome into the sanctuaries of our fellowship of believers. The question I kept asking myself was, "Now that the issue has begun to be raised, where do we go from here?"

I was still contemplating all of these questions one Tuesday morning, as I sat quietly with a small group of people who shared a contemplative prayer time once a week at a nearby Catholic Church. The priest always closed our quiet time with some kind of reflection. This particular morning he told us a story from the mythological Knights of the Round Table. "This is the story of Sir Galahad," he began. "The scene is set around a crude wooden table—round, of course. All the places are occupied by brave and noble knights. Food and drink are being consumed and there is electricity in the air. The knights are being loud and boisterous, bragging and sharing stories of victorious days gone by," he continued. "Only one knight, Sir Galahad, remains silent, drinking and eating alone in a mood of contemplation. He stays in his high-backed wooden chair long after the other knights have left in pursuit of their anticipated quests. Finally, he rises, gathers up the bundle of supplies for his trip, and proceeds to the edge of the forest. He finds the place that is the most densely overgrown with trees. He knows this way will be difficult. He takes a deep breath, grips his sword in anticipation of unknown dragons, and enters the dark forest where there is no path."

With no further explanation, the priest dismissed us with a nod and a smile and we went our separate ways.

I had no doubt that each of us in the prayer group went away with a different meaning for the mythological tale we'd heard together. I knew that the story, for me, was about dealing with homosexuality and the church. There is no clear-cut path in dealing with homosexuality in that setting. There are many unanswered questions and not a great deal of conclusive information or absolute answers available. However, if we are to be true to the principles of reconciliation, being brothers and sisters in Christ, we have to take the risk. We have to take the journey through the dark forest and into the light. Not everyone's path will be the same. At times, paths will meet. Sometimes they will collide, but we have to go forward in faith.

I wasn't sure how that could be accomplished but I had to try. I made an appointment for the next day with John, our minister, and Carla, our Christian education coordinator.

"John," I began, " I've been thinking a lot about the need for our church to begin dealing with homosexuality. There are lots of reasons to do that but one of the main ones is to get the issue out in the open so that if any of our families are dealing with it personally, they might feel comfortable asking for some support. What's your comfort level on this whole thing?"

"Actually, I've done some reading about homosexuality and have tried to work through some of the questions for my own growth but haven't put together any kind of plan to study it on a churchwide scale. Do you have something specific in mind?"

"Have you ever come across this book in any of your reading?" I held up a copy of *Is the Homosexual My Neighbor? Another Christian View* by Letha Scanzoli and Virginia Mollenkott (Harper San Francisco).

"As a matter of fact, I have. I even met one of the authors at a conference I attended a while back. It's a great book, easy to read and informative."

Carla took the book from my hand and looked at it for a minute. "It looks interesting. What did you have in mind for this, a small group study during the week or a Sunday school class?"

"I don't really know. What do you think?"

"It seems to me that the place to take this would be to the Adult Task Force. They might have some suggestions. Are you comfortable presenting this to them?"

I hesitated for just a minute, "When's the meeting? I guess it's time to step all the way out of the closet."

She gave me the date and the time of the next meeting so I could mark it on my calendar.

I'm not sure how many times I rehearsed my speech on how I had to be completely honest with the committee about why I thought doing this book study was important—that the Eric they thought they knew all these years was gay. The butterfly had always been an important Christian symbol for me, but the ones in my stomach were making me feel especially uncomfortable. When my time to speak came, I told the committee my personal story and my hopes for raising awareness in the Trinity community through doing this book study. Then I just sat there in the silence that followed. A friend on the committee winked her support to me and then an older man on the committee stood up. I wondered what was coming.

"Let me give you a hug, Beverly. That had to be hard for you to share with us. I've known and loved Eric since he was just a little guy and that will never change. I always give him a big hug when he's home to visit and I still will. I have to admit, homosexuality has been a taboo subject for me before, but now that I know it's Eric we're talking about, it puts a whole new perspective on it. Maybe we do need to take a look at this."

I was surprised at the positive response and greatly relieved. I wasn't sure if everyone else was shocked into compliance or really open to the project but I wasn't going to argue.

The committee agreed to do the book study but felt like a "test run" would be helpful. The Adult Task Force, along with a committee formed specifically to look at the issue of studying homosexuality at Trinity, spent six weeks studying the book I suggested. John presented the biblical parts of the material and I presented the rest. Everyone seemed to feel that it was well spent time and effort.

Two of the participants in the class were also the senior high Sunday school teachers. One of them stopped me in the hall after the class was over and shared some thoughts with me.

"Beverly, I hadn't really thought about this before, but since I've taken this class, I think we might need to do a unit on homosexuality for our youth on Sunday morning. I'm still not sure about all of my feelings concerning the issue, but I do know we are called to give our youth a safe and nurturing place in our church family. Just talking about it would let the kids know we are open. It might help to dispell some fears and prejudices for the students, too. We could cover the medical and scientific aspects, what the scriptures say and maybe the personal angle. Would you and Dale be willing to come talk to the youth?"

I told her I thought she had a great idea and that we would be more than happy to help.

When the time came to set the curriculum for fall of 1993, the committee felt the negative attitudes about homosexuality were probably rooted in a deeper discomfort with sexuality in general. As a result, all adult Sunday school classes were combined to do a study of *Between Two Gardens: Reflections on Sexuality and Religious Experience* by James B. Nelson (Pilgrim Press, 1983).

This book covered many areas of sexuality and included the religious and historical background that had helped us form our current attitudes. The subject matter covered not only attitudes but also ethics concerning singleness in the church, the family, homosexuality, abortion, and spirit and body in medical care. The participants in the class enjoyed some lively discussions and seemed generally receptive to some new ways of looking at pertinent issues. With the study successfully completed, I was content to sit back for awhile. I wasn't really sure where to go next, anyway.

That question was answered for me by a lady who was the chaplain at a small Lutheran college in a town fifteen miles from my home. My phone rang one afternoon and when I answered a lady named Noni was on the other end of the line.

"Beverly, your name was given to me as a possible speaker at a 'teach-in' being sponsored by our religion department."

I couldn't imagine what she was talking about. "I don't understand, Noni. Could you tell me more?"

"I'm sorry. Let me explain. As you might know, the Evangelical Lutheran Church has done an extensive study on homosexuality to try to establish its stand on the issue. We are attempting to address this with our students on campus. The goal of the 'teach-in' is to give students information with which they can struggle and formulate their own ideas and ethics concerning different sexual orientations. There are three parts to the proposed program. First, there will be a social worker / counselor who will talk about societies' difficulty in dealing with people who are different. The second part will be personal stories, that's where you come in."

"You want me to talk about our family's story—share with students? Will there be other people there, in addition to the students?" Public speaking terrified me.

"There will be some interested people from the community. You would share the stage with a lesbian woman and a gay man who would tell their stories from those perspectives."

"What's the third part of the format?"

"We have two professors of ethics and religion lined up to debate the opposing sides of scripture concerning homosexuality."

When she told me who the professors were, my curiosity outweighed my fear of speaking. They were two men I had great respect for and a curiosity about what they had to say.

"Do you need some time to think about it?"

I was afraid if I took time to think about it, I'd back out so I didn't give myself that option.

"No, go ahead and put my name down. I'll try it." I'd say "yes" now and worry about the consequences later.

She said she would be sending me a packet with the details soon.

This was the second denomination I'd run across lately that was attempting to educate people by having some kind of workshop. I had already attended a series of four programs on homosexuality the previous spring at a local Presbyterian church. Their committee had set up four lectures dealing with different aspects of homosexuality. The first was a presentation of where the Presbyterian Church as a whole stood on the issue; the second was what medical and genetic studies had shown about the possible causes of being gay; the third was a personal testimony from a family dealing with having a gay son; and at the fourth session, a video called *Maybe We're Talking About a Different God* was shown. It was about a lesbian minister who was denied her ordination in the Presbyterian Church because she was "out."

I had found their series helpful and informative but was anxious to compare it with this Lutheran "teach-in" format. There hadn't been much opportunity for discussion at the first one and I thought that might be helpful.

Finally, the appointed day arrived. Those of us who were to speak sat together in the audience waiting for the opening speaker to get the program started.

The social worker began the conference by relating the story of an event she had witnessed before her decision to go into social work. It took place in an emergency room where a gay man came in with serious heart problems. His lover was deliberately kept from his side with an official policy allowing only immediate family admittance. She said the act was clearly one of prejudice and cruelty. The sick man died alone. This event had been a large part of why she'd gone into social work. The rest of her talk was related to learning to deal with our differences.

I was the first to tell my personal story. It ended up being much easier than I thought it would be. I gave the credit to one of those popular guardian angel pins I'd stuck on my lapel and the support of a good friend who was sitting in the audience. The crowd, in general, listened as if they were sincerely interested.

When the young lady who was a lesbian gave her talk, she had some difficulty getting through the part of her story where she had experienced rejection from her family. The audience seemed genuinely empathetic as she took a moment to recover and continue.

As I'd expected, the presentations on what the scriptures had to say were interesting and insightful. The most interesting insight came later, however, when I was visiting with the professor who had presented the case against homosexuality.

"The scriptures against homosexuality all make perfect sense to me when I just study the words, but when I see the pain in the faces of people like that young woman who spoke, I have a hard time."

I think we all experienced compassion in different ways through the event.

About a month after experiencing the workshop from the Lutheran perspective, I had an opportunity to attend a different seminar with Carla, who was always looking for ways to learn more about things that might help her in the church's educational department. The one-day seminar was being offered in our area by a Catholic organization based in New York, The Center for Homophobia Education. This organization does "state tours," presenting their material several times in various locations. The seminars are led by Robert Nugent, SDS, who holds a Masters in Religious Studies from the Catholic University of Louvain and Jeannine Gramick, SSND, who holds a Ph.D in Education from the University of Pennsylvania. The seminar is titled "Building Bridges: Gay and Lesbian Christians and the Church."

We arrived at the seminar just in time to register, pick up our materials, and find a seat.

Jeannine Gramick opened the seminar by telling why she was there. Some twenty years before she had developed a friendship with a young man who was gay. She'd been so strongly affected by that friendship and the young man's story that she'd since devoted her life to promoting education about, understanding toward, and acceptance of gay and lesbian people.

Robert Nugent, in his presentation, pointed out that oppressed people look at God from the perspective of their own experience. With that in mind, he shared some interesting observations. A gay person who feels that being gay is a sin is looking for repentance. Someone who feels like he or she is sick is looking for healing. When the oppressed feels like an outsider, justice or social activism may be the focus. The person who feels like his or her orientation is natural is looking for a place to use whatever special gifts he or she has to offer. In this atmosphere people are able to flourish and grow.

I whispered to Carla, "Aren't we are all like that to some degree?"

She nodded in agreement.

All points were interesting to me but I especially liked the last one. As Christians looking at gay and lesbian ministry, we often look only at "ministering to" and not "ministering with" those gays who are a part of our fellowship.

As Mr. Nugent talked about models for ministry, it became evident that three specifics were important. "The law lends itself to ministry for civil rights; the medical field is open to a ministry with AIDS support and counseling; and the area of religion is open in many ways for pastoral care, family support, and spiritual nurturing. Individuals, professionals, and churches have a variety of opportunities to serve in any of these areas of need."

We closed with an activity that proved extremely helpful. In small group discussions, we were to put ourselves in lesbians' and gay persons' shoes. We were given specific family, social, moral, and ethical situations and asked to look at them from a homosexual viewpoint, on the other side of the fence. It turned out to be an exercise in compassion for each of us.

I thought the workshop was helpful and I wanted to make sure I had their address for future reference. I copied it off the chalkboard: The Center for Homophobia Education, P.O. Box 1985, New York, N.Y. 10159 (301/927-8766).

Up to this time, I had been involved in programs organized and presented by the Presbyterian Church, the Lutheran Church, and the Catholic Church. I wanted to know what was available through my own United Methodist denomination.

As luck would have it, I would have that material practically fall into my lap. Our family was having a delayed Christmas at our daughter's in St. Paul, Minnesota, in late January, 1994. Dale had a professional meeting in Minneapolis, the second reason we were in the Twin Cities. Traci was at work and Eric was exploring Minneapolis with a friend. I was in our hotel room planning my day. I decided to make some phone calls to see if I could find out about what was going on in this part of the country with the gay issue.

I called a Methodist church that I knew to be involved in studying the issue in hopes of becoming a Reconciling Congregation. The woman I talked to was delighted by my interest.

"There's a study out that was put together by a task force in the Minnesota Methodist Conference. It's called *Faithful Inquiry—Exploring Christian Responses to Homosexual Persons*. All the churches in this conference are doing the study sometime during the next year. We've been into it for three weeks and are finding it informative and helpful. Let me give you the address of our conference office. You can get a copy there for eight dollars."

I jotted down the information: The Minnesota Annual Conference, United Methodist Church, 122 West Franklin Ave., Minneapolis, MN 55404.

The conference office just happened to be within walking distance of our hotel room so I made the short trip down the block and bought three copies.

When I read the study in detail, I found it to be thorough, balanced in presenting all viewpoints, nonthreatening, and true to what the title stated as the purpose, exploring Christian responses to homosexual persons.

The study is made up of six one-and-a-half-hour sessions or ten one-hour sessions: (1) Talking about sexuality in the church: why it's difficult, why it's necessary; (2) Walking in someone else's shoes; (3) Sexual orientation; (4) Interpreting scripture; (5) Examining homophobia: evidence, effects; (6) Models for ministry.

Each session had easy instructions for the facilitator and activities for the participants. The study set the tone for dialogue and left room for everyone's feelings and opinions. A helpful bibliography for further reading was included at the end.

I talked to a young man who is the coordinator of the Reconciling program of another Methodist Church in Minneapolis about the study and he believed it had opened doors to a much broader understanding in their community.

I could hardly wait to get home to see how we might use this study at Trinity. I gave my three copies of the study to John, Carla, and the chairperson of the Adult Education Task Force. They all looked at the material and agreed it would be a good study to do in our church, but I still had a sense of restlessness for some reason. I gave it some thought, and called John and Carla to meet again for further discussion.

I shared with them some of the things I'd been mulling over in my mind. "You know, I've been thinking about our doing the study on homosexuality and I know it's needed but I wonder if we need to look a little further than that. Maybe we need to look at what the church is really about on the whole. We would be doing a disservice to what Jesus taught about hospitality and inclusiveness if we dealt with only one group of people."

John smiled a knowing smile and shared his feelings with us. "We must have been on the same wavelength, Beverly. I've been wanting to preach a series of sermons on "building bridges" for some time now. That's perfect. We can cover bridges to the poor, bridges to the hungry, bridges to persons of color, other religions and on and on. I'm getting excited. Carla, what do you think?"

"We can have a churchwide theme and look for materials for all levels from little children to the adults. There is information out there that will help us all understand people of different races, different cultures, different family configurations—the possibilities are unlimited. Everyone will be thinking inclusiveness at the same time. I'm excited too."

In the fall of 1994, we did our "Building Bridges" series. In one of the adult Sunday school classes we reviewed the sermon that had been preached each previous Sunday. Many people shared that the challenges presented in the sermons had caused them to "stretch" their faith and rethink their current attitudes and actions toward others. In one sermon, John shared a dream he had for our church.

"I want to be able to look on the front pew in worship and see an ultra-conservative fundamentalist Christian, sitting next to a liberal-left Christian, sitting next to an anti-abortionist, sitting next to a pro-life person, sitting next to a homophobic person, next to a gay man—next to a gay man!—all worshiping together. That's my dream for Trinity."

At the same time that John preached on "building bridges," our lay leader and I taught *Faithful Inquiry* in six Sunday afternoon sessions. We had twenty-three participants who all said they found the study enlightening, informative, and imperative to their Christian growth. They recommended that we give it again in the spring, which we did.

At Trinity, our hope is that this process has helped us all to come a little closer to understanding how to live in a diverse world with an attitude of love, hospitality, and inclusiveness as Jesus did in his lifetime.

And so, we, the Christian community, start our journey, like Sir Galahad, at a dark place by the edge of the forest. We don't know what dragons the knight in the story had to slay or what perils he met along the way. For us, though, as Christians making new paths for living our faith in a complex world, there are perils we need to be aware of, especially in dealing with homosexuality. The dragons of fear, stereotypes, prejudices, and old religious baggage might prove to be too heavy a load on our way to forging new paths through the forest. We may have to let go of some things as we travel. We do know, however, that when we come to the jagged ravines along the way, God will provide bridges for us so we can reach the other side.

22

Go in Peace

Over the last decade I have seen families of gays in all stages of emotional adjustment and degrees of involvement in their own healing. My heart goes out to them, as I know they have a tough journey ahead of them. I always try to encourage them to take that journey, not to give up, but to grow with what has been given them in life. I tell them to stand behind their gay child, to support him in making a good life for himself and the others he'll be associated with throughout his lifetime. I do this because as I look back on my own life, I see the changes this experience has made for me, either in reinforcing things in my life that needed to be reinforced or in establishing new things that needed to be in place.

Many positive things have developed from having a gay son. Some of what I've learned has helped me to grow personally, to become a stronger person. Other lessons have been spiritual. Those lessons I cherish most.

The experiences having to do with relationships have been the most rewarding and inspiring. It's been a joy to see my husband and two adult children grow in their appreciation of people's diversity. I realize what a gift I have in a supportive husband who, unlike so many men, is not homophobic. I have a new love and respect for my parents, as they've had the courage to journey with us toward understanding. The ministers and personal friends who have stood by our family and supported us have given new meaning to the words *love* and *friendship*. We have also found acceptance in our larger faith community, the one I doubted in the beginning. The association I've had with the beautiful gay and lesbian people I've met has been a real blessing.

All three areas—personal, spiritual, and relational—have been full of life-giving, positive insights that have made my life better. It is my hope that the content of this book has enhanced the lives of its readers, as well.

Probably the most important lesson I've learned in the course of the last several years has been to look behind the labels society tends to put on groups of people, to see the real individuals. In the process of learning to understand and accept gay people and to appreciate their diversity, I was awakened to the uniqueness of all people in the world around me. For a variety of reasons, we seem to need to make judgments as to what is desirable and acceptable in people. We use criteria ranging from race and gender to body size and shape, to eye slant and color. We judge one another by how much money we have or don't have, by social standing and political party. Even different religious groups fuss and try to prove each other's thinking wrong.

God tried to make it easy. He sent Jesus to take care of our sins so that we could just love him and each other. What should be simple remains nearly impossible.

All of these thoughts were going around in my mind one morning when I was soaking in the bathtub, trying to come up with a piece to write for my church Lenten booklet. As my thoughts began to come together, I realized how many ways we judge each other and how much that judgment gets in the way of the peace Jesus wished for his people on this earth. I knew then what I wanted to say. I got out of the tub, dried off, and threw on my bathrobe. I went to the computer, and this is what I wrote. With this piece, and in *peace*, I end my story and wish you well.

Go in Peace

There is a sign hanging in the back room of the bookstore where I work. It reads, "What would Jesus do?" When I find myself struggling with what is right or wrong on a particular issue, I visualize that sign. When you think about it, most problems in our lives deal with people and relationships. One of the big things that gets in the way of relationships in our society is the need to label and categorize people. Then we decide if their label fits what we think is OK. Jesus didn't do that. Here is a story I put together to illustrate what could happen if we followed his example.

A worldwide Easter service had been arranged, and Jesus was the guest speaker. A huge cathedral was erected, complete with padded pews and elaborate stained-glass windows. A United Nations Task Force had appointed greeters to stand at the cathedral doors and hand out name tags. The name tags were huge because everyone entering was to fill them out with information set up in the guidelines of the Easter worship service committee.

"Please indicate whether you are black or white, male or female, Christian or Buddhist, rich or poor, gay or straight, conservative or liberal, saved or sinner…and so on," the greeters instructed.

The congregation was dressed in its finest and on its best behavior. Expectations were high. Would they hear another Sermon on the Mount, or witness a miracle?

Of course, the Reverend Billy Graham had been chosen to introduce Jesus. His introduction was simple and to the point.

When Jesus stood up and approached the podium, you could have heard a pin drop. No one dared breathe.

Jesus looked out over the crowd in silence for a moment, and then he spoke these simple words. "I died for each and every one of you. God loves you that much and I love you that much. Now, go and love each other."

Then he sat down.

Was that all? People weren't sure what to do. They looked at Jesus and then they looked at each other. As they exchanged glances, there in the crowded pews, they began to notice something. The huge name tags that had been so full of information were now blank. Everyone in the room was the same; equal. No one could identify the differences anymore. They were seeing each other as God sees them.

The room filled with love and light. The people linked arms as Billy Graham stood up, raised his hands, and said, "Go in Peace."

Epilogue
Love Casts Out Fear

It has been twenty-two years since I first overheard that fateful conversation from the top of my basement stairs. On that night, approaching Christmas in 1985, I thought our life was going to be changed forever, and not in a good way. I had a son who was gay, a way of being that I knew nothing about--a way of being that even caused concern for Eric, himself. I remember asking Eric if he thought a single, lifelong friend of ours might be a lesbian. He immediately responded with this comment, "Oh, no! She's too good a person." That was my first clue that he was afraid that some dark and scary lifestyle might lay ahead for him as a gay person. That made me sad and afraid.

He also voiced the concern that he wouldn't be able to be gay and Christian--that somehow those two ways of being weren't compatible, and he couldn't change being gay. That broke my heart. My own personal Christian faith, along with my faith community, had accompanied me on my spiritual journey while supporting me through many of life's trials. Eric was feeling deserted by God and that same faith community. I found myself afraid to voice the pain caused by a subject that I thought was off limits for the Church.

Fortunately for both of us, we found pastoral support behind closed doors in the office of the minister. Eric continued to participate in youth group and youth choir. That provided some sense of normalcy during a time when he felt like he was someone very different from his peers.

Many fears came bubbling to the surface of my mother's worry tank during this time. I was concerned that Eric would never have a meaningful relationship--one of monogamy and commitment, but would wander from one empty relationship to another.

I was afraid for his safety in a world of unjustified hate and prejudice. I even secretly harbored my own fear and prejudice against those who had HIV and AIDS, while being terrified that we might someday be dealing with the dreaded disease in our own family.

Eric was going to be pursuing a career in theater. Would the casting couch be a threat for males as well as females? Would anyone turn down his request for employment because he was gay?

Even though we were a close family, I feared tension between family members because of this new dynamic that we didn't understand. We had always said we'd love our children no matter what. Did we really mean it?

The fear that weighed heaviest on my heart was that Eric would find rejection from the church that he had always loved. He had learned the lessons of how to feed his own spirit, of how to love other people, and how to love in the world in a way that was kind and helpful. I wasn't seeing any signs of affirmation at this time in the life of the larger Church Denomination for folks who were homosexual in their orientation. I did find myself playing the "grace" card I'd been hearing about from the pulpit my entire life. I was wondering if my church family was dealing from the same deck or would they lay down the "judgment" card? It felt really risky to throw all of our cards on the table for everyone to see.

The problem with being stuck in a place of fear is that it makes your life very heavy and you always move in slow motion. At one time I had knelt at the church altar and pledged my life to God--promising to live my life in an attitude of love to the best of my ability, always looking to the life of Jesus for guidance. My heart was telling me that Jesus loved each member of my family equally and wanted to continue to be in relationship with them. A heavy, slow motion, self-centered life wasn't conducive to acting on that commitment.

When I became more educated on the subject of homosexuality, the fears began to subside. As I observed my son living his life with the same kindness, integrity, and ethical behavior I had appreciated before I knew his secret, I began to regain my confidence. I even sat in the pews at church and took in the love and support I needed from friends in my congregation who I felt would support me if they knew I was hurting. But, because Eric was still in high school, I felt like I couldn't put him in a position of vulnerability by saying anything to anyone.

Over the next ten years, after Eric had gone to college, I started "coming out" to both personal friends and family and family at church. To my relief, the responses were positive and supportive. Eventually, I asked our adult task force to offer some classes on sexuality and spirituality that included a positive spin on homosexuality. A friend and I offered a series exploring what the Church's response to homosexual persons should be. All were well received. I even found out that other people in the church had gay relatives. We helped each other look at those relatives with new eyes and more enlightened hearts.

In the meantime, Eric was finding opportunities to meet and date other gay men during the course of his theater studies in college. He dated in the same manner as his heterosexual counterparts, one at a time and in social situations. There were times when he experienced some harassment from other students on campus, but he learned to handle the comments with a sense of humor--a skill that proved helpful on several occasions. .

My husband and I became active in a parent support group that was eventually moved to our church building when the original site was no longer available to our group. It helped to hear other family stories--both trials and victories.

Eventually, I was challenged to author this book. At first I was hesitant, but grew into finishing the project and finding a publisher. The terror that followed the acceptance of the manuscript caught me off guard. I fell into the trap of thinking I had to become a flag-waving, button-wearing, gay-pride-parade-marching person to be an advocate. I thought that was the image that went with being the person who had written this book. Although it might be comfortable for some other advocates, that style didn't fit my personality. Personal friends and professional counselor friends eventually helped me see that all I needed to do was be myself and tell our story. As I look back, I find it kind of amusing that I was pushing so hard for people to accept homosexuals as they were, but I thought I had to be somebody besides myself to support them.

When it came time to publish *Cleaning Closets* I asked Eric if he was having second thoughts about our personal lives being out there for all to see. By this time he was finished with college and was in New York following his theater bliss. He said, "Heavens no, Mom. I'm going to set up a table in Time Square and sell them to everyone who comes by!" That was in 1995.

As I write this epilogue, the calendar pages are showing that Christmas is fast approaching again. It will be the Christmas of 2006. A lot has happened in the last twenty-two years.

Eric was able to follow his dream of being a professional actor for a number of years. He did numerous seasons of summer stock, both while in college and later during his time in New York. He spent nearly two years with a theater company in California before moving on to New York where he spent close to three years practicing his craft. During those years he had a role in a Disney movie and played the synthesizer for the Broadway show "Grease." However, in 1996, Eric decided he was tired of the theater rat race and headed to Los Angeles as a civilian.

By now, thanks to a young lady who had been part of the cast of a Christmas show he'd done in Oregon, he had reconnected with his spiritual roots, but he wasn't sure where that would take him. A friend suggested he visit his church, an interesting mix of Eastern and Western religions. The church emphasized meditation and the services were filled with chanting and singing. The scriptures that were read were from the holy books of both Hinduism and Christianity. Everything in Eric's apartment became saturated with the smell if incense. This time served as a transition time in Eric's faith journey.

Los Angeles wasn't really a good fit for Eric. He couldn't find work that he liked, the relationship he was in wasn't going well, and he was in mourning for his acting career.

As luck would have it, I got a brochure in the mail advertising a workshop on the labyrinth, a meditative walking path, at San Francisco's Grace Cathedral. Eric loved to meditate and walk the labyrinth. I sent in the registration and mailed the details to Eric for his birthday.

It turned out to be exactly what Eric needed, He stayed with a theater friend, Michael, who told him that if he didn't like Los Angeles he should move to San Francisco. Jobs were plentiful and he could stay with him. That's exactly what Eric did.

One of the first jobs Eric had was in a bookstore that furnished volunteers for a program that provided meals for the homeless. It was sponsored by the Metropolitan Community Church in the Castro, the gay section of the city.

On his day off, Eric would go to the church and help prepare and serve meals. It was there that he met, Joe, a volunteer on staff at the church. They went to dinner and then began to date on a regular basis.

Joe and Eric clicked immediately and were soon established as a couple. Eric was to bring Joe home to meet the family in the summer of '98. They laughed because Joe is fifteen years older than Eric and he didn't know what to call us because he was closer to our age than Eric's. We settled on

Mom and Dad. A few days before they were to arrive we got a phone call from Eric. He said he needed to be upfront with us because Joe would be in our home and we would probably see him taking a lot of pills. "Joe is HIV positive, Mom. We just thought you should know."

I tried to say something in response, but I had no voice. I thought we had dodged the bullet that was the last of my fears, HIV and AIDS. Now Eric was in a committed monogamous relationship and I thought he was safe. I was talking on the phone, six feet from the laundry room where I'd first found out Eric was gay, and the panic was back.

"Mom, don't worry. We have talked to the doctor and we can be together and be safe. It just takes a few precautions."

"Okay. Are you sure? Never mind. We'll see you next week."

Once I regained my composure, I told myself that there was nothing I could do about this situation. I had worked through finding out Eric was gay and now I found out the person he loved is HIV positive. Maybe this would help me take a closer look at my own prejudice. So often we keep our heads buried in the sand until an issue becomes personal, and now HIV was touching our lives in a very personal way.

We were instantly taken by Joe's warm personality and good looks when we finally got to meet him. We could see why Eric had fallen for him. A part of me was proud of Eric for loving Joe, no matter what. Joe shared that he'd been HIV positive for twenty-five years and had done very well on his medications. His continued good health was one of the reasons he felt so passionate about his call to the ministry. He felt like God had work for him to do. One of those tasks would be to gently teach his new family some lessons they needed to learn--learn by his example of living with HIV himself and the compassion the disease had taught him in dealing with others.

As I thought more about it, I became more hopeful. What if Joe had had cancer? Was this any different? I would hope Eric wouldn't leave someone he loved just because there was an illness involved. They said they would do everything they could to keep Eric safe. I had to let it go and just take each day as it came. It was obvious how happy they were.

In November of 2000, our entire family went to Africa on an eye care mission. Eric and Joe, our daughter Traci, Dale and I were all together. When we arrived at our hotel in Nairobi, Traci and Joe headed for the newsstand. They were looking for news about the now infamous "hanging chads" from the Florida elections and information on who had won the

Big Twelve football national championship title. Joe and Traci are huge football fans. At one point I saw Traci go over to Joe and give him a big hug and say, "I'm glad you're going to be my brother-in-law!"

In February of 2001, Eric and Joe were joined in what they refer to and what we experienced as a wedding in the church where they met. It was a moving ceremony in which our entire family participated. Joe had family take part, as well. We immediately felt connected to Joe's family. When I show the happy couple's video to friends they say it is one of the most beautiful ceremonies they have ever seen. We agree. The following day, Joe was ordained as a MCC minister.

Joe now pastors a congregation of his own. Eric is very active in that congregation. We feel so fortunate that they have a supportive, life-giving faith community to be a part of--a place to grow in their relationships with God and each other.

Unfortunately, as I write this epilogue, most of the mainstream churches are still debating the issue of homosexuality. Some are saying they are open to people of all sexual orientations, but have refused to open the doors to pastoral ordination and the celebration of same-gender couples' relationships. Some still call homosexuality a sin. A few have instituted reparative programs to help gays become straight. I feel that this is unfortunate--a social justice issue. I've heard and been moved by so many wonderful and yes, some tragic faith stories from the gay community in the last twenty-two years.

Their stories have been the inspiration for my second book, *Voices from the Kingdom: All God's Children Have Keys*. In this book, gay and lesbian Christians, Christian parents of gay children, and advocate pastors and bishops tell their faith stories around the issue of homosexuality and the Church. It is because of people and stories like those found in the pages of this work that I have learned that love really does cast out fear. Instead of being something to fear, the experiences we have had in getting to know people in the gay community have been a treasured blessing for which we are sincerely grateful.

For Further Reading and Reaching Out

The following list of resources range from conservative to liberal thinking on the subject of homosexuality. The texts range in degree from somewhat conditional to totally unconditional acceptance in dealing with homosexuality and the persons having that orientation. This variety in resources is deliberate as readers' needs and backgrounds tend to vary widely on this subject. Each resource does, however, have positive insights to offer and I invite the reader to explore the material with an open mind, seeking broader understanding of gays and each other.

There was not space in this book to deal specifically with "coming out" but resources containing full or partial focus on that aspect of homosexuality are marked with an asterisk (*).

*Back, Gloria Guss. *Are You Still My Mother? Are You Still My Family?* New York: Warner Books, Inc., 1985. (Good for anyone, but especially families of gays.)

Barbo, Beverly. *The Walking Wounded.* Lindsborg, KS: Carlsons', 1987. (A mother's true story of her son's homosexuality and eventual AIDS-related death.)

Bawer, Bruce. *A Place at the Table: The Gay Individual in American Society.* New York: Poseidon Press, 1993. (A conservative gay man bridges the gap between straights and gays and helps society learn.)

*Bess, Howard H. *Pastor I Am Gay.* Palmer Publishing Company, 1995. (An American Baptist Pastor shares his journey as he ministers to gays and lesbians)

*Borhek, Mary V. *Coming Out to Parents: A Two-Way Survival Guide for Lesbians and Gay Men and Their Parents.* New York: Pilgrim Press, 1983. (Helpful for gays and lesbians and their families in dealing with each other's feelings during the "coming out" period.)

Borhek, Mary V. *My Son Eric: A Mother Struggles to Accept Her Gay Son and Discovers Herself.* New York: Pilgrim Press, 1979.

Boswell, John. *Christianity, Social Tolerance, and Homosexuality.* Chicago: University of Chicago Press, 1980. (History of gay people in Western Europe from the beginning of the Christian era to the fourteenth century. Contains an excellent chapter on scripture.)

Cook, Ann Thompson. *And God Loves Each One.* A publication of the Task Force on Reconciliation, Dumbarton Methodist Church, 3133 Dumbarton Street, N.W. Washington, DC 20007. (Good general publication for understanding.)

*Eichberg, Rob, PhD. *Coming Out: An Act of Love: An Inspiring Call to Action for Gay Men, Lesbians, and Those Who Care.* New York: Plume, 1990. (Outlines, step by step, the best way to come out of the closet in a positive and powerful way. Includes letters from workshop participants.)

Fairchild, Betty and Hayward, Nancy. *Now That You Know: What Every Parent Should Know About Homosexuality.* Harcourt Brace Jovanovich, 1979. (Good general information. Positive steps to take in going forward.)

Fortunato, John E. *Embracing the Exile: Healing Journeys of Gay Christians.* New York: Harper Collins, 1982. (Stories of the spiritual struggle and growth of gay Christians told by a gay psychotherapist.)

Furnish, Victor Paul. *The Moral Teaching of Paul: Selected Issues.* Nashville: Abingdon, 1979. (Specifically, Chapter III. A more detailed look at the Bible scriptures concerning homosexuality and the morality of other Christian issues.)

Garden, Nancy. *Annie on My Mind* (fiction), New York: Farrar, Straus and Giroux, 1982. (The story of two girls who begin their relationship as friends and discover they are more to each other. Well done.)

Glaser, Chris. *Coming Out to God: Prayers for Lesbians and Gay Men and Our Families, Friends and Advocates,* Louisville, KY: Westminster/John Knox Press, 1991. (A beautiful collection of prayers dealing with Christian faith in connection with homosexuality and other issues of social acceptance.)

Glaser, Chris. *Uncommon Calling: A Gay Man's Struggle to Serve the Church,* New York: Harper Collins, 1988.

Griffin, Carolyn Welch and Wirth, Marian J. and Arthur G. *Beyond Acceptance: Parents of Lesbians and Gays Talk About Their Experiences,* New York:

Prentice Hall, 1983. (Parents talk about what comes after acceptance of homosexuality.)

Hilton, Bruce. *Can Homophobia Be Cured? Wrestling with Questions That Challenge the Church,* Nashville: Abingdon, 1992. (A focus on the difficult questions Christians raise about the diverse issues connected with homosexuality.)

Hopke, Robert H. *Jung, Jungians, and Homosexuality,* Boston: Shambhala, 1991. (A technical book about what Jung and Jungian psychologists have to say about homosexuality.)

Hostetler, Helen M. *A Time to Love: When AIDS Takes a Son, a Friend,* Scottdale, PA: Herald Press, 1992. (A mother's story of her struggle and anguish as she loses her son to AIDS. A spiritual journey.)

Johnson, Barbara. *Where Does a Mother Go to Resign?* Minneapolis, MN: Bethany House Publishers, 1979. (A mother's story of how her Christian faith took her through many traumas. Strong faith story—conservative viewpoint—filled with unconditional love.)

Marcus, Eric. *Is It a Choice? Answers to Three Hundred of the Most Frequently Asked Questions About Gays and Lesbians,* New York: Harper Collins, 1993. (Honest answers to questions about homosexuality. Good resource.)

Nelson, James B. *Between Two Gardens: Reflections on Sexuality and Religious Experience,* New York: Pilgrim Press, 1983. (A general look at past, present, and future attitudes on sexuality in the church. Excellent resource.)

Open Hands. Journal of the Reconciling Congregation Program, P.O. Box 23636, Washington, DC 20026.

Polk, David P., editor. *Now What's a Christian to Do?* St Louis: Chalice Press, 1994. (Stirs serious thought and lively discussion on tough, contemporary issues including prayer, homosexuality, teenage sexuality, suicide, and more.)

Rogers, Jack. Jesus, the Bible and Homosexuality: Explode the Myths, Heal the Church. Louisville, Kentucky: John Knox Press 2006 (A Presbyterian, Evangelical minister and professor takes a look at the Bible to argue for the full inclusion of gay and lesbian people in the church and to heal the church)

Roscoe, Will. *The Zuni Man-Woman,* Albuquerque: University of New Mexico Press, 1991. (The story of the sacred place homosexuals have in Indian culture. It is about We-wha, a Zuni man-woman.)

Scanzoni, Letha and Mollenkott, Virginia. *Is the Homosexual My Neighbor? Another Christian View,* San Francisco: Harper and Row, 1978. (Thought-provoking, insightful thinking about homosexuality and the Christian faith.

*Silverstein, Dr. Charles. *A Family Matter: A Parent's Guide to Homosexuality,* New York: McGraw Hill, 1977. (Helpful general information written by a psychologist.)

Readers who wish to contact Beverly Cole may do so by writing:
Beverly Cole, PO Box 358, Salina, KS 67402-0358 or info@kimimipub.com

Beverly Cole is a wife, a mother, and a church woman. As Christian and the mother of a gay son, she has worked as an educator, an advocate, and a supporter for the gay community in society and in the Church. She works nationally with the Reconciling Parents Network of the United Methodist Church and is coordinator for that organization in the Kansas West Conference.

Beverly has told their family story to numerous Church, university, professional and civic groups. She does sensitivity training for the local Hotline in the area of homosexuality and homophobia. *Cleaning Closets: A Mother's Story* has been featured on the United Methodist Women's international reading list of recommended reading for the Church.

Kansas is home for Beverly, her husband, Dale, and their three cats, Smokey, Cassie, and Janet. Beverly enjoys spending time with her daughter, Traci, and traveling to visit her son, Eric, and his partner, Joe. In her spare time, she relaxes by reading, gardening and also hiking in places where her husband can capture nature with his camera.

Also available from Kimimi Publications:

Voices from the Kingdom: All God's Children Have Keys

"That's the dumbest thing I've ever heard!"

It was in a moment of complete and utter despair that Sue heard God's response to her lament that she didn't think she could be gay and Christian. It's a theme that surfaces numerous times within many of the stories told through *Voices from the Kingdom: All God's Children Have Keys.*

The body of the mainstream institutional church has been so busy debating the issue of whether or not homosexuality is a sin that the faithful voices of our gay brothers and sisters can barely be heard above the roar of the conflict. If we listen, there is wisdom to be shared from the gay community, culled out from the struggle with the Church's condemnation. There is an abundance of compassion served up in response to the threat of rejection. Moments of humor cover up the tears.

Take spiritual journeys with Sue and other gay and lesbian Christians, advocate parents, pastors and bishops. You'll find it impossible to ignore their voices when you hear their stories.

Religious Groups Supporting Open Faith Communities

Affirmation-Mormon
Affirmation
Gay and Lesbian Mormons
PO Box 46022
 Los Angeles, CA 90046-0022
 Phone-1-661-367-2421
 www.affirmation.org

United Methodist Affirmation
Affirmation
United Methodists for Lesbian/Gay
Concerns
PO Box 1021,
Evanston, IL 60204
umaffirmation@yahoo.com

American Baptists Concerned
American Baptists Concerned
PO Box 3183
Walnut Creek, CA 94598
www.rainbowbaptists.org

Brethren Mennonite Council for
Gay Concerns
Brethren Mennonite Council for
Gay Concerns
PO Box 6300
Minneapolis, MN 55406
Phone-1-612-343-2060
bmc@bmclgbt.org

Dignity (Catholic)
Dignity
1500 Massachusetts Ave NW
Suite 8
Washington DC 20005
Phone-1 800-877-8797
Phone-1-202-861-0017
info@dignityusa.org

Friends for Lesbian, Gay, Bisexual,
Transgender, and Queer Concerns
(Quaker)
Newsletter
c/o Sue Sierra
1314 Wright Street
Ann Arbor MI 48105
www.quaker.org/flgbtqc

GLAD Alliance-Gay and Lesbian
Affirming Disciples (Disciples of
Christ)
GLAD Alliance
PO Box 44400
Indianapolis, IN 46244-0400
glad@gladalliance.org

Integrity- (Episcopal)
Integrity
620 Park Ave # 311
Rochester, NY 14607-2943
Phone-1-800-462-9498
info@integrityusa.org

Lutherans Concerned/North
America
Lutherans Concerned/North
America
PO Box 4707
St. Paul, MN 55104-0707
Phone-1-651-665-0861
www.lcna.org/contact.shtm

Presbyterians for Lesbian/Gay
Concerns
More Light Presbyterians
PMB 246
4737 County Rd. 101
Minnetanka, MN 55345-2634
www.mlp.org

Reconciling Ministries Network
(United Methodist)
3801 N Keeler Ave
Chicago IL 60641
Phone-1-773-736-5526
www.rmnetwork.org

Unitarian Universalist Office of
Lesbian/Gay Concerns
Unitarian Universalist Association
25 Beacon St
Boston, MA 02108
Phone- 1-617-742-2100
info@uua.org

Universal Fellowship of
Metropolitan Community Churches
MCC Churches
PO Box 691728
W. Hollywood, CA 90069
Phone- 1-310-360-8640
info@mcchurch.net

Praise for Cleaning Closets: A Mother's Story

Led by her heart and her mind, this faithful mother decides to explore many different perspectives in order to more fully understand same-sex attraction and how it relates to spirituality, as well as to ease her own intense anxieties. From the biblical vantage point to the psychological and personal, her education becomes our education. The manner in which it is written is warm and inviting.

For those parents or children who are just "coming out" of their own "closets"—indeed for anyone who is grappling with the implications for their faith of God's unabashed love for gay men and lesbians—I enthusiastically recommend it.

Allen Harris-Developer of Open and Affirming Congregations and writer for Disciple Magazine

PFLAG parents will find that the book covers much familiar ground, but it is uncommonly gratifying to read an account that describes so many positive experiences in both church and community. Her church, through Beverly's leadership, sponsored a series of workshops on the theme of "Building Bridges," which helped to develop understanding among its members. The book includes information about programs and projects sponsored by other churches.

The Lawrence, Kansas Chapter of PFLAG